*Nicole, May my testimony be a blessing to you.*

# GIVEN BEAUTY

# FOR

# ASHES

*When Beauty Emerges from the*

*Ashes of Darkness*

Nicole,

May my testimony
be a blessing to you.

4/10/16

# GIVEN BEAUTY

# FOR

# ASHES

*When Beauty Emerges from the*

*Ashes of Darkness*

**Tamika Marie**

For information regarding bulk purchases of this
book, digital purchase and special discounts, please
contact the Author.

**Printed in the United States of America**
Cover Photo Design: Visionary Designz
www.visionarydesignz.com

Editor: LPW Editing & Consulting Services, LLC
www.litapward.com

First Printing, 2018
**ISBN:** 978-0-692-65161-2

# Dedication

This book is dedicated to my amazing daughters, Kevyona and TeMariona Chappell. You both are my double blessing, my precious diamonds, and my motivation. I would not be who I am today without you girls and I am blessed that God chose me to be your mother. My prayer is that you both will honor God with your whole heart, mind, body, and soul. Put God first in all you do so that He will direct the paths you take. May this book be encouragement for you and the generations to come. This is just the beginning of deliverance and breaking generational curses off our family. Mommy loves you the most and we win!

# Acknowledgements

First and foremost, I want to thank my Heavenly Father. Jesus Christ, thank you for loving me enough to die for me so that I can live. This book was written out of obedience, for Your glory and I know You are proud. I thank You for calling me out of darkness and into Your marvelous light. I look forward to this journey with You.

To my mother, Ivy Jones: Mom, I thank God that He formed me in your womb — I would not be here if it wasn't for you. You are such a strong woman and I've watched you overcome the many things that life has thrown your way. I thank you for all you have done and are doing in my and your grandchildren's lives. I love you mommy!

To my siblings: Bonora, Dominique, Tiara and Joel: You all are the next generation of believers that will have to lead your friends, daughters, sons, nieces and nephews to Christ. It is time to lead them down the right path. I thank you for loving me and I am grateful for the bond we share individually and collectively. I love you all very much.

To my cousins/best friends: Centhla and Lanise, thank you for your obedience as God called you by name. It is from there God began to raise us out of darkness. Thank you for being there through the highs and lows as God chose us to change and make a shift in this generation. I thank God for allowing us to go through this together. You both are wise beyond your years and I appreciate your gifts of encouragement. Continue to allow our Father to use you both mightily. I love you both so much!

Colleen and Toviaz: You ladies are amazing and you have no idea how God used you to help me write this book. Colleen, you said "Tamika when you move to North Carolina, write a book." Toviaz you said, "You will write books, and you will be a best-selling author." If it wasn't for these confirmations, this book would not exist, so I thank you!

To the born-again believer: It is not enough to just be born again. After God has called you out of the darkness of this world, cleansed you and forgiven you of your sins, there is much work to do. The Holy Spirit desires to use you to save lives as He did with you. Our duty is to save souls for Christ. It is time to rise up and get serious for the Lord. The bible says, "The harvest is plentiful, but the laborers are few." It is time for us to truly be about our Father's business. Let's get to work!

# TABLE OF CONTENTS

# Introduction

I was crying my eyes out while sitting in the bathtub of our two-bedroom home. I received a denial letter that same day regarding a car loan I was sure I was going to be approved for. It felt like I was losing everything right before my eyes. James was in prison, I was having a tough time keeping up with the rent, and my car was totaled in a car accident that happened a few weeks earlier. I felt hopeless and alone and like I had hit rock bottom. I sat in the bathtub feeling sorry for myself with a cigar in my left hand and a beer in my right. I felt like I had endured more than I could handle at 27 and life couldn't get any worse. With James incarcerated for the next three and a half years, I had to begin handling everything on my own. I was trying to be supportive of him and our daughters, physically, mentally, emotionally and financially. At the same time, I was trying to remember to take care of myself.

Suddenly in the midst of my tears, something happened inside of me. I was finally awake and knew I needed to stop feeling bad for myself. I finally realized I needed to start doing better. I was now a single mother of two beautiful four-year-old twin girls that were looking up to me. I needed to be that example not just for them to strive to do better in life, but also for them to do better than me. I realized that I was the oldest of four siblings that were struggling to find their way through life. I needed to be a positive influence for them to make it through. My mother struggled so hard and sacrificed so much to do the best she could for us. Although she did not graduate from high school, I needed to be the one to show her that she raised us to be better in life. She implanted strength in us as she overcame her struggles and it was time for me to be better than her. I was still sitting in the bathtub, alone with my thoughts. I had no idea that God was calling me in that moment and was ready for me to live out my purpose in life. When I finally got out of the bathtub, I sat down in front of my laptop. I began to type about my life not realizing God was beginning to birth something within me. Not knowing He was going to use my life story to share with the world.

In January of 2013, I had taken my first trip to visit North Carolina and was planning to move there. After returning from my visit, I received my first confirmation from God regarding Him wanting me to write this book. I recall the day I was at work, when a co-worker I had become very close to said to me "Tamika when you move to North Carolina, you need to write a book." I laughed and told her I thought it was funny that she would say that because I had just began typing about my life several months prior.

Then in June of 2013, I received my final confirmation while sitting in the bishop's office of my church. I was a month away from moving to North Carolina with my cousins and my daughters. We were having a meeting with bishop regarding the move, when a woman entered the room. She began to ask bishop questions regarding a brief announcement she wanted to give during church service on the following Sunday. She knew my cousin and was aware of us moving to North Carolina. While she was in the office, she began to share a testimony of her moving to Minnesota from New Orleans. Suddenly, she began to prophesy to my cousin. When she was finished with her, she began to prophesy to me. She declared to me, "You're going to be a bestselling author. You are going to write books. I want you to look at the palms of your hands and see the many people that are waiting for you." She also told me not to worry about what people may say or be ashamed. In that moment, I ran out of the office and cried because I knew God was speaking to me through this woman. I had no idea that those pages I typed a year before would turn into a book or that the meeting in Bishop's office would become one of many divine moments in my life.

I wrote this book out of obedience to what the Spirit of the Lord was saying to me. Many people have life stories to share that will help break the chains off many others. The Word of God in Revelations 12:11 says, "And they overcame him by the blood of the lamb and by the word of their testimony." This is my testimony and life story that God is using to overcome the enemy and for Him to get all the Glory!

# Chapter 1

# My Silent Journey

*I* was born on the Southside of Chicago, Illinois, at Mercy Hospital on March 11th, 1985. I remember my mother telling me that we lived near the Ida B. Wells Projects on the "low end" of Chicago off 39$^{th}$ Street and Ellis Avenue. Growing up in the projects, my mother, along with her three sisters and two brothers, was exposed to gang activity and joined gangs at very young ages. My mother being the baby of the bunch gained the nickname "Baby G" and was a Folks gang member. She told me that months after she had given birth to me, she nearly lost her life when a group of gang members attacked her. This attack left her with severe injuries from being hit with a pole against her head and knees. Apparently, this attack was set up by a woman from another gang because my mother was involved with another man, other than my father. My little sister, whom I will refer to as Denise, and I were raised there until I was nine years old. However, those years were mostly filled with bad memories.

Denise and I had two different fathers; mine died from a heart attack when I was about three years old and Denise's father was not in the picture. Soon after my father passed away, our mother started struggling with a drug addiction.

She used to hang out at a friend's house where they would smoke joints together. The house had a back room that her friend warned her about. She told my mother about the drugs people in there were using were much stronger than the joints she was accustomed to smoking. One day, curiosity got the best of her and she went into that back room. She tried her first hit of crack cocaine and was hooked. It eventually became an addiction that she battled for years. Although my mother was on drugs, she desired to overcome her addiction but she struggled to do that while trying to take care of my sister and me. My mother entrusted one of our aunts to take care of us until she got clean and could care for us herself. I was six years old when my mom put us in the care of our aunt.

When the crack epidemic hit the projects, one of my aunts moved to Minnesota with her boyfriend. My grandmother and the rest of our family soon followed her to Minnesota and my mother was transferred to a drug rehabilitation center there. Denise and I were still in my aunt's care when we moved but she became so sick that she was put in the hospital. One day when my mother came to visit my sister and me, she arrived at my aunt's house and was told that we were sent back to Chicago and placed in foster care. My mother had no idea my aunt was hospitalized. She expressed the anger and hurt that she felt showing up to her sister's home and being told that we were taken away and no other family members had taken us in.

I remember the day the foster care worker came to pick

us up from my aunt's home. Although I was six years old, I was old enough to know what was happening and that she was there to take us away. I remember crying, kicking, and screaming as she took us from my aunt's home. It was one of the toughest experiences for a child. Denise and I were in the foster care system for three years; we were placed in three different foster homes but thankfully were able to stay together the entire time. While in the first two foster homes, I remember getting into trouble for doing things I knew I was not supposed to do. I guess you could say it was a way of me rebelling. Could you blame me? There we were, living in a home with people that we did not know. It was as if we were in a foreign country being held against our will. Ironically, the third foster home turned out to be the home of the grandmother of my uncle's girlfriend, Mama JJ. It was not until I was older that I realized God's hand was over our lives the entire time.

Mama JJ was a sweet older woman; she was also a Jehovah's Witness. The foster family we lived with prior to moving to Mama JJ had us attending a Baptist church. Jehovah's Witness church was a bit different because we didn't celebrate certain holidays and I remember attending big Jehovah's Witness church conventions throughout the year. We attended church service majority of the week. On the weekends, my uncle's girlfriend would pick Denise and me up to spend time with her. She would curl our hair and put our hair in pretty, colorful banana clips, which made me feel like we were finally around family.

Then, we started having supervised visits with our mother. Although my mother was still completing her treatment classes, Mama JJ allowed her to visit us often. I was happy to be able to see her more, but it wasn't good enough. I still had an empty place in my heart that needed to be filled with my mother's presence permanently. Every night when Mama JJ would have us pray before bed, I would always pray for us to be back with our mother.

My mother fought hard for us to get back into her custody. She was at a better place in her life; she was clean and had completed her treatment classes. She was married by then with a new life in Minnesota and two other children. I remember the day Denise and I were sitting outside of the courtroom waiting for my mother and Mama JJ. I was nine years old at the time and I knew this day would determine whether we were going to be back in our mother's custody. I remember praying outside of the courtroom, asking God to bring us back together with our mother for good.

One day while I was in school, I saw my mother and her husband walking into my classroom. She picked me up in her arms and told me that we were coming home to Minnesota with her. I hugged her so tightly! God heard my cry at the tender age of nine and answered my prayers.

Moving to Minnesota was bittersweet for me. After three years of being away from my mother, we were now with my family for good. We were now starting this new life. It was no longer just Denise and I because our mother had other children. We had two sisters, I will call them

Jeanette and Rochelle. Not too long after, our little brother, who I will refer to as Jay, was born.

Growing up, I envied my other two sisters and brother for having their father in their lives while Denise and I did not. Their father, who was also our mother's husband, accepted us as his own daughters. Although he accepted us as his own, I never really felt comfortable calling him dad. He was a very heavy drinker and would frequently get into arguments and physical fights with our mother.

Although I had no memories of my father, I always felt it would be disrespectful to call another man my father because my dad is deceased. My mother would constantly remind me of how much I favored my father in my looks and characteristics. Apparently, my father had a habit of balling up his toes, something I would do often. My mother told me I had other sisters and brothers on my father's side and I was the youngest of my father's children. After my father died, my mother tried keeping in contact with them, but said that they had a difficult time accepting me as their father's child since he was so much older than my mother was. They could not fathom their father, who was fifty years old, would have been involved with my mother who was seventeen years old at the time I was born. Years later, we were able to get in contact with one of my uncles on my father's side of the family. We visited him in Chicago once when I was about ten years old. He shared stories about my father and said how much I looked like him. But that was the first and last time I had seen or heard from him.

I hated being the oldest. I always had the responsibility of watching my younger siblings and I really didn't like them at the time. Don't get me wrong, I loved my siblings but I could not move past the mounds of bitterness and envy in my heart. I was put in a position to not only accept siblings I barely knew, but also having to acknowledge my mother's husband as my father. Although I was having these issues, I never expressed how I felt to my mother and silently kept them bottled up inside, ready to explode.

As a couple years went by, I had so much bitterness built up. I took it out on my sisters and brother when my mother wasn't around. I remember choking one of my sisters because I was so angry and bitter towards them. It had always been just Denise and I, but now I was the oldest of five, which was a lot of responsibility. I was four years older than Denise was and she was three years older than Rochelle. Rochelle was a year older than Jeanette, while Jeanette and Jay were three years apart.

My mother had always wanted a boy; my brother could get away with anything since she favored him over us. I don't think she realized just how differently she treated us individually. Jeanette was the baby girl so she was treated like Jay, able to get away with anything because she was the baby girl. Rochelle was also favored due to her being my mother's "sick child". She was sick frequently, including a time she was so sick that she had to have her appendix removed at an early age. But she was the middle child so she just blamed everything on Denise and me or Jeanette and

Jay. Then there was Denise; she eventually turned into the "black sheep" of the family. I think she took the move to Minnesota much harder because it was always just the two of us. With Denise, suddenly being older than three other kids, life got extremely hard for her. She would get whippings all the time. It seemed that she was blamed for everything our siblings would do.

My mom counted on me a lot since I was the oldest and I had a lot of responsibilities at the age of eleven going twelve. She and her husband would leave forcing me to oversee my siblings when they were gone. One day, I went into my mother's room to find a movie for us to watch and while looking for a movie, I came across a blank VHS tape. I wasn't sure what it was so I put it inside of my mother's VCR player and what I saw next changed my life from that day forward. There was a man and woman doing things on that video that my eleven-year-old eyes should not have seen. A curiosity was sparked inside of me and there were things going on in the video that seemed too familiar to me. The images on the video brought back a memory of an incident I experienced while living in one of the foster homes.

At first, I thought the incident was just a dream that my mind would not allow me to forget, but it was actually a memory I had learned to suppress over the years. It was a memory of me playing with Barbie dolls in the bedroom with an older girl that was the daughter of a foster parent we were living with when I was six or seven. I would frequently have the image of her having me do things that I should not have been exposed to. After watching that video, something happened that made me aware of certain things I should not have been feeling. From that moment, I was curious to figure out exactly what they were doing in that video. My curiosity became worse when I found out my uncle owned a store where he sold the same type of videos, which I later learned were pornography videos. He was my favorite uncle because he spoiled all of his nieces and nephews. He was always the "rich" uncle in the family. He would bring all of us over to his home and spoil us rotten. He would buy us all kinds of toys, give us money and we would have so much fun.

One weekend, my uncle left me in charge while he left to run errands. He had a closet full of pornography videos. I grabbed one and put it in the VCR in one of the bedrooms as my sisters and cousin were playing in another room. While I was watching the video, Jeanette came in the room. I didn't think she knew what I was watching because she was four years old at the time, so I let her stay. Then Rochelle and my cousin Tiffany came in the room. They were all younger than I was, so I didn't think they really knew what we were watching, but I was wrong.

When the weekend was over, my mother came to pick us up from my uncle's home. During the ride home, Rochelle started telling my mother about the movie I was watching. She tried to explain what the man in the video was doing to the woman but I panicked. I tried to say it was a scary movie and the bad man was "hurting the woman" in the movie. When my mother asked my cousin Tiffany about the movie I was watching, I knew I was in trouble. She told her and my mother was appalled. She told my aunties and my uncle all about it. I couldn't hide from the embarrassment. It was a long time before I watched another video, but it was too late. Watching those forbidden videos opened the door to an addiction to pornography and masturbation that would last for the next 16 years.

# Chapter 2

## Living in Discomfort

My mother and her husband always provided for my siblings, and I. We always had a beautiful home and we had never lacked anything. My mother was a homemaker, but an interior designer at heart. She would always decorate the house with beautiful furniture. The dining room table was covered with beautiful tablecloths. There would be dishes on the table that no one could use, with marbles in each dish. We had a china cabinet filled with beautiful dishes that were only for decoration.

My mother would decorate my sisters' and brother's bedrooms with new bedroom sets. She would put different Disney characters on their walls and paint the walls pretty colors. I had my own bedroom with a vanity table and chair with lights at the top of the mirror that made me feel like a movie star. I had a windowpane in my room that I would sit on a lot listening to songs like "Sitting up in my room" by Brandy while watching a boy that went by the name "Red" across the street that I grew to have a crush on. My mother would give me gold earrings, necklaces and even gave me a gold diamond ring that I wore on my left ring finger. The ring was so beautiful and resembled a wedding ring so much that when I was in the fifth grade, a teacher asked me if I was married. My mother would always tell me I was married to her and instructed me to never remove the ring from my finger. When I wore that ring, I had a sense of importance, of value.

My mother began to move us a lot while I was still in elementary school. She and her husband continued getting into fights that became extremely physical. Oone of their fights was so bad that my mother stabbed him multiple times in self defense. He survived and did not press charges against my mom, but this time she packed up our things and moved us to a shelter. We lived on the Southside of Minneapolis and then we moved to the Northside. We even stayed in the suburbs of Cottage Grove and White Bear Lake for short periods. I felt as if I was attending a different school every year. I would get comfortable at a school, begin making friends and then we would move again. While attending an elementary school in White Bear Lake, there were majority of white students attending the school. I had become very popular after the R&B group Backstreet released a song called "No Diggity." A verse in the song says, "Tamika's in full effect" so a lot of the students in school thought my name was cool to be mentioned in a song. I had gained a lot of friends because of it, but this was short lived. Just when I felt like I was sitting on top of the world, things in our lives took a turn from bad to worse.

Since leaving Chicago, we had never lacked anything. However, I knew things weren't okay when my mother and I pulled up to a building one morning for an appointment.

Before getting out of the car, she stated that she needed me to go into the office and act the opposite of the well-mannered child she taught me to be. She pretty much wanted me to act as if I had no home training so she would be approved to receive a Supplemental Security Income (SSI) check.

As I walked into the office with my mother, I was nervous because I really didn't know what to do. So, I started messing with papers in the office as the woman we met with spoke to my mom. The woman would ask me to stop and I would, but I would get back up to mess with other things in her office. After the appointment, there were times I would be pulled out of math class, which would later have a tremendous effect on my math skills. During class, I had to meet with someone from the agency who would test me to determine whether my mother should receive the SSI check. For instance, they would show me a picture of a car and I would say it was a chair. I was a very smart girl so it was hard for me to act stupid. It was so obvious that the person from the agency asked me if someone was making me do it and I said no fearing they would take me away from my mother again. Needless to say, she was not approved for the check. I believe my mother was just trying to find a way to provide for us. It may not have been the best decision to make, but I also believe it was a result of our environment. Some other family members had gotten approved for SSI checks, so she was only trying to survive the same way as those around her. While in the fifth grade, my mother ended up moving me to another school and we began staying in another shelter.

Harriet Tubman was the name of the shelter we moved into on the Southside of Minneapolis. The shelter also had apartments attached to the other side of it. Living in shelter after shelter was completely different from what I was used to. We always had our own house and I always had my own bedroom. But in the shelter, we had to share our room with people we did not know and would even share the same food. My mother found out one of my cousins and her mother lived in the apartment side of the shelter. The rule was that no one from the shelter could go over to the apartments. However, my mother allowed me to sneak over to their apartment while she stayed in the shelter with my younger siblings. I would pack up my little Tweety Bird backpack and go through the bottom level of the shelter to get over to my cousin Clar's apartment. I would spend the night at their apartment a lot and I loved being there because it was better than sleeping in a room with strangers. Although I didn't like living in a shelter, the staff cared for the lives of those living there, and would even put on different events. One particular event I will never forget was when all the children in the shelter were brought together to sing a song by Whitney Houston called "The Greatest Love of All". After we were finished, each of us were asked to share what we wanted to be when we grew up. When it was my baby sister Jeanette's turn, she stood up in front of everyone with confidence and said, "I want to be a piece of pie!" which caused everyone to burst out in laughter. Moments like these brought joy to such an unstable time of our lives.

After living in the shelter for a while, we moved in with my grandmother who had an apartment in Minneapolis. I don't recall my mother ever sharing with me why we were moving so much, but I remember never feeling comfortable. I was attending another new school and only had two outfits to wear for a whole week. One outfit was a plaid long sleeve shirt with jeans and the other was a sweater with black corduroy pants. I would switch pieces of the outfits by wearing the sweater with jeans, and then the plaid shirt with corduroy pants hoping my classmates would not notice me wearing the same two outfits. My mother's husband was a truck driver and travelled to many different states. We were living in the shelter because my mother was trying to get away from him; but she must have kept in contact with him because somehow he convinced her to move us to Florida. Once he told her he found a house for us, she moved us in with our grandmother to prepare for moving out of state.

Many years later, my mother shared with me that she had also received a lump sum of money from my father's pension during the time we were preparing to move to Florida. A few days before moving, she took me to get my hair braided at an African Hair Braiding shop and bought me new outfits. After wearing the same two outfits throughout the week, I walked into class the last two days before we moved with my head held high as my classmates complimented me on my hair and clothes.

~

It was my first time riding an airplane as we flew into Florida. Eustis, Florida was such a beautiful place and I loved seeing the tall pine trees as we drove, while embracing the warm weather. As we pulled up to our new home, I remember my mother being very upset. The house was not very nice looking on the outside. The first thing I noticed, walking into the home, were the wires hanging out of the wall. The house was rundown and my mom refused to move us into it.

After staying in a hotel for a few days, her husband had an aunt by the name of Auntie Bee whom we were able to stay with until they found us a home. My mother even considered moving us into a mobile home that was just as big as a regular home. But we eventually found a nice home that we moved into and were finally able to get comfortable. My mother got us settled in school and we even started attending church. I remember one Sunday my siblings, my mother and I were all dressed in white linen and were baptized. Everyone seemed nice at the church and my mother became friends with a woman from church who began tailoring my mother's clothing. She had one older son and two daughters. One of her daughters was around my age and I would go over to their home to hang out with her.

One day while I was over their house, I was in their bathroom when I began to hear screaming outside the bathroom door. When I opened the door, my friend's brother was on the carpet rolling as fire covered many areas on his body. He had set himself on fire by pouring fuel all over his body and sparked a match onto his skin. As he got up yelling, I stood there in shock seeing pieces of his skin hanging off. Although the fire was completely out, he ran outside feeling as if he was still on fire. Their mother was not home at the time, so the older sister put my friend and me in the back of their truck as she got in the driver's seat. She pulled up to their brother who was running down the street. She got him to get into the truck and drove him to the hospital. He was covered with second and third degree burns. His sister said he had tried to kill himself in the past and I believe he was only about sixteen years old. After witnessing something so traumatic, I don't recall my mother ever letting me go back over to their house.

My mother and her husband were back getting into their usual arguments. They both were getting drunk and fighting each other, but this one almost cost my mother her life for the second time. My mother later shared with me that they were arguing while he was driving. She said he was threatening to take her somewhere to harm her, so she grabbed the wheel of the car. This caused them to swerve off the road, crashing into a tree and left my mother in a coma while in the hospital. Luckily, my siblings and I were at home when this happened. We stayed with Auntie Bee while she was there, she told me my mother was hurt in a car accident but we didn't know she was in a coma at the time.

After she recovered from the coma, she came home with a brace around her neck. I believe my mother was fed up and that accident was her wake-up call. My mother also mentioned one of her sisters back in Minnesota needed her help. So, after six months of living in Florida, we were heading back to Minnesota but our journey back was not so smooth. We ended up staying in another shelter along the way. But we were only there for a brief period of time. My mother got in touch with her brother who had a house in the suburbs of Chicago. So, he let us stay with him for a little while until we made it back to Minnesota.

When we made it back to Minnesota, we moved in with one of my aunts until my mother got us an apartment in Brooklyn Center. I was entering the sixth grade when I started attending Northeast Middle School, which was in Northeast Minneapolis when we moved to Brooklyn Center. To prevent me from having to switch schools, my mother allowed me to stay at my aunt's home during the weekdays and I would go home to Brooklyn Center on the weekends. This worked in my favor because my mom's sister that needed her help, asked if she could let three of her children stay in our bedroom apartment. When I would come home on the weekends, the apartment was crowded with us sharing beds and making pallets on the floor. Consequently, I was happy to stay at my aunt's home where I had my own bed.

My aunt's daughter, who I will call Na'Kei, and I attended the same middle school and grew very close. My

Aunt attended Zion Baptist church in North Minneapolis. She always had us in church or doing something that was church related. Na'Kei was a praise dancer and she sung in the choir. I would go to church with them but I never really got involved. I was too busy being boy crazy and having the freedom to do what I wanted while away from my mother's house during the week.

Na'Kei and I would hang out at the local recreational center that was down the street from her house and even joined the recreational center's dance team. We would hang out at the basketball court with our older cousin Reece, who started staying at my aunt's house too. Reece was much older than I was but she was like an older sister. Her boyfriend stayed in the apartments across the street from my aunt's house, but there was a boy who lived in those same apartments that I really liked.

He was a couple years older than me when we started hanging out and asked me to be his girlfriend. He was so sweet to me and this was something I had never experienced. We never did any of those things from the images of porn that were embedded in my mind. We would walk to the park together holding hands; he would hold me and I had my first kiss with him. However, being someone's girlfriend was something I had not yet understood. I say this because since elementary school, while having a "boyfriend" I would also have interest in another boy at the same time. So, when he asked me to be his girlfriend, I said yes but I also liked another boy who was friends with him. I liked his friend a lot too so I ended up writing him a letter to tell him. He showed the letter to my then boyfriend and he was crushed. I was very hurt from the situation because I didn't mean to hurt him and he never spoke to me again. For a while, I did not have interest in other boys, but the memory of those pornography videos would still flood my mind.

# Chapter 3

# Who Am I?

During middle school, I wore my hair with my signature swooped bang and a side ponytail. I dressed in oversized overalls and t-shirts. Although I was a tomboy, I was an A/B honor roll student and I received awards for being the student of the month multiple times. Back then boys weren't interested in having me as a girlfriend; they were more interested in knowing where I got my clothes. I would wear oversized shirts from clothing lines such as, FUBU, Karl Kani and Enyce, just to name a few. But as I went on to seventh grade, there was a boy I grew to have a crush on. One day, I got up enough courage and wrote him a letter explaining how I felt about him. I remember him saying to me in the school hallway that he liked me too. But he didn't want to date me because his friends said my teeth were yellow and crooked. My feelings were hurt and I began to view myself differently and started to compare myself with the other girls in school. To make matters worse, I was diagnosed with Juvenile Gum Disease Gingivitis. I was only thirteen years old when the dentist told my mother I could lose my teeth by the age of twenty-three. I began to have low self-esteem and felt rejected. I no longer thought I was pretty and the ring my mother gave me slowly began to lose its value.

As I entered the eighth grade, there was a girl who became popular in my school. I would overhear boys saying they wanted her as their girlfriend. In typical middle school fashion, I started to compare myself to her. As time went on, I started styling my hair the same way she did and dressing the same way she dressed. Immediately, boys took notice of me and I liked the attention I was getting. I even had a boy in my apartment complex that wanted to date me. Before you know it, my mother allowed me to have my first date with him. We dated up until I graduated from middle school and moved to Saint Paul, which is where I entered my first year at Arlington Senior High School. While I was staying with my aunt, I attended church service with her and was involved in different events through the local Salvation Army. However, when we moved to Saint Paul, we attended church services only on holidays such as Easter and Mother's Day. During this time, the relationship I had developed with God as a child had become nonexistent and I eventually stopped praying to Him all together.

As I think back to my first year in high school, it was a challenge for me at first. My mother moved us to a new city and I didn't know anyone at the time. I was shy and intimidated by the older students. Some students would even give me a tough time and wouldn't make room for me in the seats on the school bus. I began wearing my oversized jerseys again and wearing my hair with the swooped bang up until I became friends with a girl at school. She was everything I wasn't. She was very girly and there was not a shy bone in her body. She was born and raised in Saint Paul, so she knew a lot of the other students. Throughout my ninth and tenth grade years, we were inseparable. She had completely changed me from this tomboy that wore big herringbone chains with oversized t-shirts, into wearing fitted tops and jeans. We would dress alike at times and we hung out with the same friends. But in the middle of our tenth grade year, she moved and could no longer attend Arlington. By that time, I had formed my own circle of friends. Just as I was turning sixteen, I started working at a hotel as a suite attendant, cleaning rooms on the weekends. I also joined the cheerleading team at school and would cheer at games on school nights. I would purposely make it home just as everyone was going to bed. I tried to do anything that would keep me away from the house just so that I would not have to hear my mother arguing with her husband or my sisters getting in trouble.

I can't remember actually when masturbation became a habit for me. It was a seed that had grown tremendously since I first watched the pornography video when I was eleven. There were times I would go into the bathroom and touch where no eleven year old should know to touch. I started feeling sensations that I later learned were orgasms. It then became a habit for me to lock myself in the bathroom or my bedroom just to feel the same way I had felt that first time. One day, a boy cousin came over to our house. He was slightly younger than I was and I knew there was something wrong with him mentally. I had him come in my room where

I touched his private part and rubbed it against mine just to have an orgasm. I felt so guilty and knew that what I had done was beyond wrong. I pleaded with him not to tell anyone, and I never did it again.

As the years went by, masturbating and watching porn became something I did regularly throughout middle school and high school. It had gotten so bad that I would buy pornography movies on the cable box in my mother's home. Once she started to notice someone purchasing the movies, I stopped. I don't believe she ever thought I was buying the movies since she never approached me about them. However, that never stopped me from staying up late at night to watch after dark shows on HBO like Red Shoe Diaries. Pornography movies seemed to always be within my reach. One of my older cousins had a boyfriend who was open about watching them. I would take different pornography videos, while looking through their movies and eventually had my own collection. Masturbation was something I became immune to doing. The habit was so bad that when I was tired, I would masturbate just to wake up. There were even times that I would masturbate just to have a good night of sleep. The pornography movies opened me up to a world of curiosity and promiscuity. Around thirteen years old, my mother was not home and one of my cousins was over with a friend. We were all having a water balloon fight, when my cousin's friend who was about sixteen or seventeen years old told me how he liked the outfit I had on. From that day forward, I wanted to be around him more.

One night, while everyone else was playing a game of hide and go seek, he and I ran off with each other to hide. He showed me things I remembered from those familiar pornography videos. This led to multiple encounters with him where I almost lost my virginity, but something inside of me would not allow me to go further.

I never revealed to anyone about the things I was doing. My mom had so much going on with her and my siblings. Denise was getting whippings so much that my mother started leaving welts on her back. She eventually rebelled against my mother. She started smoking cigarettes around the age of twelve, had boys calling the house, and began running away from home. It also got to the point where I didn't think the fighting between my mom and her husband would ever stop. They were fighting so much that I don't think she realized her children were spiraling out of control.

Eventually, she got tired of the fights and so was I. One night as the living room in our house reeked of cigarettes and alcohol, my mother and her husband began fighting. I was so tired of it that I ran over to him and jumped on his back to stop him from hitting my mother. That was the night she decided she would finally file for a divorce. After our mother got the divorce, she started dating another man. Rochelle did not like him and started becoming rebellious by picking arguments with him and our mom. On top of that, my mother would hear about Denise and what she was doing out in the streets. She started drinking heavy and calling her once precious daughter everything else but her name. She would spout on about how fast my sisters were; yet labeled me as her "only good child." She felt I didn't do any of the things they were doing. Although my mom didn't whip me or call me out of my name the way she did my sisters, I still hated being home.

I don't recall my mom ever talking to me about the birds and the bees. But I had already known how it felt to be at second base with a guy before entering high school. There were times I wanted to tell her about the things I was doing but never did due to fear. I knew if I told her, she would attempt to beat it out of me. Deep down inside, I knew what I was doing was wrong, but I kept it to myself. I believe my encounters with boys, along with my addiction to pornography and masturbation, led me to make many careless decisions throughout my years in middle school and high school. The seed continued to grow within me as I entered high school, which eventually led me to lose my most prized possession at the age of sixteen… my virginity.

My addiction to pornography and masturbation had become much worse. There were times I would be working at the hotel and would purchase pornography movies in the rooms and watch them as I masturbated. A year later, I transferred to bussing tables at the breakfast and bar area. I would come straight from school to work. There were nights the bar area was very slow and I would already be exhausted from being in school all day. So, I would go into the bathroom to masturbate just to give myself energy.

During my junior year, my cousin Tiffany started

attending Arlington and we began hanging out more. She was two years younger than I was and on a well-known drill team in Saint Paul and she knew everybody. During this time, there was a guy who showed interest in me and we started dating. He was a few years older than I was and I was in love or so I thought.

Tiffany was best friends with his younger cousin, so she and I became friends as well. She lived a few blocks away from my house so we would spend most of our weekends hanging out at her house. There would be house parties there all the time. People were drinking alcohol and smoking marijuana, but I was not into any of that at the time. I was there because he was there and I was happy to be his girlfriend. He was very popular in Saint Paul and was a part of a gang called "The Rolling 60's Crips." I was so young and naïve. I was willing to be his ride or die chick; I even held a weapon and drugs for him. I was only sixteen years old when I lost my virginity to him. As I look back, I can't believe I was thinking a twenty year old man, was in love with me the way I was in love with him. I eventually started hearing about him being with other girls and even heard he was dating one of Tiffany's older sisters, which was my cousin! I was livid, I was hurt, and I was so embarrassed. However, once I confronted him about it, he denied everything...and I believed him.

Throughout high school, I continued the relationship with him. When he violated his probation, and had to spend a few months in jail, I was right by his side. I would send money for whatever he needed such as, clothes, shoes, and even money towards a television. I would drive with his cousin to the prison on weekends to see him. But I was still hearing rumors of him having other girlfriends and was told he was sending letters to my cousin. Tiffany and his cousin knew exactly what was going on, but didn't want to get in the middle of it. I didn't want to believe it, so I continued settling for his attention knowing deep down inside it was being shared with my own blood cousin. I was hurting on the inside and wanted revenge for what he was doing. So when another guy began showing he was interested in me, I would find myself making out with him in a room called "the black box" during school. I started sleeping with different guys not knowing, at the time, that I was trying to fill a void in my heart caused by the hurt I felt from the man I thought I loved. I became a complete mess emotionally.

I never revealed to my mother about what was going on because she didn't even know I wasn't a virgin anymore. Everything that I went through, I kept bottled up inside. My mother had so much to deal with regarding my siblings that I didn't want to be another problem for her. A year passed and I was still working at the hotel after school all while still being on the cheerleading squad. Denise ran away from my mother's house for good, Rochelle was having boys calling the house, and Jay was failing in school and staying out past curfew. It seemed that once Denise ran away, my mother no longer cared.

I never really acknowledged this new man in my

mother's life. He was a nice person and my mother seemed happy. He eventually moved in, but he and Rochelle just could never get along. I believe she never got over the fact that our mother and her father were no longer together. Denise was still gone; we were hearing rumors of her doing drugs and dating men that were twice her age. But she would check in occasionally and tell us she was doing fine. Rochelle started running away from home and Jay had teachers calling the house saying he was still failing in his classes and wasn't bringing his homework to school. Jeanette was the only one not giving my mother hell and seemed to be okay with the changes in our home.

During my senior year, I was battling many things underneath the surface. I had finally broken things off with the guy I had been with throughout high school. When he was released from prison and I found out he was still messing around with other women, I finally came to my senses. But at the same time, I was still in love with him. Because I didn't want to be with him, I continued sleeping with other guys. I would allow a guy to get close to me, have his way with me, and then push him away because he didn't fill the void I had. I was constantly in this cycle. I didn't realize that I was seeking something that was lacking inside of me that I thought could be filled by someone else. Because of this, I had a lot of "friends" that came and went.

I had a guy friend who liked me for a long time and wanted to be in a relationship with me. But I felt so damaged on the inside. I remember him saying to me, "Tamika, you are a beast and you don't even know it." The term "beast" at the time meant I was amazing and I was valuable. He was right but I did not know it, or believe it and I eventually pushed him away. One day while working in the bar area, I noticed the diamond missing in the ring my mother had given to me at eleven. I was seventeen years old as I looked down with a mound of disappointment and felt as empty as the space where the diamond once was. I took the ring off my finger because I no longer saw the value in it. In that moment, I also no longer saw any value in myself.

# Chapter 4
# The Wake-Up Call

*A*fter my senior year, I graduated and had done pretty well in school. I remember wanting to attend a historical black university to become a fashion designer. I had dreams of naming my jean clothing line "Mika j's." But I was lost and had no idea who I was anymore. I didn't know where I was going in life and started smoking marijuana heavily. I finally enrolled and started attending Century Community College in White Bear Lake for a semester. One night while driving home from work, I fell asleep behind the wheel and totaled my 1988 Plymouth Sundance. Luckily, I exited the car unharmed but my car was completely damaged. Due to not having a car, I started taking the city bus to class. It would take me three buses and a shuttle to get to and from school. Therefore, after I completed the semester, I didn't return because of the distance on public transportation.

I started partying a lot and was old enough to get into nightclubs. I would get all dressed up on the outside, but was battling low self-esteem on the inside. The girls I partied with had pretty smiles, bigger behinds, and I thought they were better looking than me. The only thing I felt was attractive about me was my thighs and hips. I believed if I wore clothes that revealed my shape and didn't show my teeth as much; guys would think I was pretty too. Sounds silly, right? But that's how I thought. My thoughts told me I was not pretty enough and that I had to sleep with guys just to get their attention. If they thought I was sexy, then I felt validated when they wanted me in their bed. I never wanted a relationship with any of the guys I slept with but I needed their attention. I needed to have someone to sleep with just to feel "loved" but not realizing that I was devaluing myself.

I met a guy that was the cousin of one of Tiffany's best friends and would always see him over her friend's house. He would flirt with me and he reminded me so much of my ex-boyfriend that I still had feelings for. He and I started seeing each other and I started to have strong feelings for him. He and I became serious. However, his cousin Kay warned me that he had a past of being abusive towards women. In the beginning, he showed no signs of it. Until one day, he and I were play fighting at a gas station. He picked me up and slammed me onto his car hard. It was to the point that the gas station clerk yelled from the intercom regarding what he had just done to me. I wasn't hurt, but I definitely took heed from that day forward.

He and I had been together for several months when I found out I was pregnant. When I told him about it, he wasn't against the pregnancy but he wasn't excited about it either. I was more worried than anything because I was only nineteen years old and had no idea what I had planned to do with my life let alone have a baby. But I was also a little excited because one of my friends was pregnant as well and we both were in the early stages of pregnancy.

One night her I had gone out to a nightclub like we usually did on the weekends. After walking around the club, we made our way to the dance floor when I noticed my boyfriend there with a group of his friends. I didn't go over to him right away because I was having such a good time. As I continued to dance with my friend, I noticed him with his hand on another girl as she had his phone in her hand. I knew by the looks of it that the girl was putting her number into his phone as she began to dance with him. I immediately walked off the dance floor full of emotion and went to the bathroom. My friend followed me as I sat in one of the stalls crying my eyes out. As she looked at me with concern, I told her what I had seen him doing and that he knew I was pregnant. She was trying to comfort me but I was so hurt and just wanted us to leave.

The nightclub was going to close soon so we left and drove to a White Castle restaurant that wasn't too far away to get something to eat. The restaurant was also one of the hang out spots everyone would go to after the clubs closed. There were already a lot of people there as we got in line to order our food. As we waited, I noticed my boyfriend walk in the door of the restaurant. He saw me and I could tell he was intoxicated. I was already irritated from what had taken place in the club, so as he approached me with a smile on his face, I was not having it. He was trying to put his arms around me but I kept pushing him away. I got so frustrated that I walked out of the restaurant. He caught up with me and was trying to talk to me but all I could do was cry and yell because of the emotions that were built up inside of me. I kept pushing him away and even walked across the street from the restaurant near some apartments just to get away from him. But he followed me and we began arguing so much that he punched one of the apartment windows. From that moment on, I knew I couldn't have a baby with him.

That night I decided I no longer wanted to be with him and that I would get an abortion. I never told him when or where I was getting the abortion. I went alone and made what I thought was the best decision at the time. However, I had no idea that I was about to destroy one of God's good and perfect gifts. After having the abortion, I remember the cab ride home being such a blur. When I got home, I laid in my bed and cried myself to sleep. I didn't tell anyone about the abortion, not even my mother, until years later.

I was drinking alcohol and smoking marijuana on a regular basis. I had become the walking lyrics to a popular rap artist's song where he said, "Once a good girl's gone bad, she's gone forever..." It became worse when Tiffany and I decided to get an apartment together. All we did was work, drink, smoke, and party. We lived in walking distance from two of the popular nightclubs in Saint Paul at the time. We would get all dressed and go out to different nightclubs at least three times a week. There were times we would take ecstasy pills or "magic mushrooms" that were called "shrooms" and would be so high off these drugs before entering the nightclubs. Once, I remember being so intoxicated before walking into a nightclub that I had to walk back home because I was too drunk to go in. I spent the next two years of my life doing the same thing, until an incident occurred that caused us to be evicted from our apartment and led us to go our separate ways.

Tiffany and I moved out of our two-bedroom apartment and into a three-bedroom with our close friend Kay. We were living in the apartment for about five months until we got evicted. The apartment was two-levels and Kay's room was upstairs. One morning, I heard Kay and her boyfriend arguing, which I had become accustomed to, so I didn't get involved. But this time was different. I heard a lot of noise and someone running out of the apartment door. As I came upstairs I could smell the weed they were smoking, but when I looked inside of her room, no one was there. I opened the door to our apartment and noticed a broken phone smashed in the hallway.

I went back into the apartment to try calling her phone from my cell phone when I heard a knock at the door. I assumed it was Kay or her boyfriend, so I opened the door. To my surprise, it was the police. They told me that they received a domestic call to our apartment. However, due to the apartment reeking of marijuana, which they could smell from the hallway, they began to enter the apartment. One of the apartment managers was walking past when she noticed the police at our apartment door. She was coming to our apartment because she was informed of the 911 call. The apartment complex had a zero tolerance for drug use so she immediately entered the apartment as well. As the police searched our place, room by room, and saw ashtrays with marijuana residue, we were evicted immediately. Everything was so surreal and I couldn't believe what was happening. My cousin was at work at the time, but I called her to tell her that we had just been evicted from our apartment. She was so angry that she hung up the phone in my face. After the police and apartment manager left, Kay finally returned to the apartment. After telling her all that had just happened, she felt so bad about it and couldn't stop apologizing. We had 72 hours to move, which led us all to go our separate ways.

I believe everything happens for a reason. That eviction needed to happen for me to stop living such a careless life. I needed a wake-up call. I wasn't going anywhere in life had become too comfortable with my lifestyle and state of being. I was too comfortable working at the hotel for almost seven years with no dreams of advancing. I was partying, drinking, smoking my life away and didn't realize that what I was doing was toxic. At one point, I came into work at 3 a.m. because I was scheduled to cook breakfast at the hotel that morning. I had been out all night partying, taking ecstasy and was still high when I arrived to work. I remember going into the bathroom to change into my work clothes. When I came out of the stall, I looked at myself in the mirror and saw that my pupils were dilated. It made me so sad because I knew that was not who I was.

I even had a "come to Jesus" moment while hanging out

with friends one night when we were all drunk. We were walking from a party and passed by a church. When I saw the church, in the midst of my drunkenness, I asked God to forgive us. I believe my friends and me even started singing a gospel song as we continued to walk down the street. You see, even in the midst of my sin, I knew I was not living right. I was too busy trying to fit in with what everybody else was doing, that I never developed into who I was supposed to be. During this same time, I started dating a guy I met at my job. After almost a year of dating, I became pregnant. When I found out it was with twins, I immediately received my wakeup call.

# Chapter 5

## Awakening Love

## Before It's Time

*J*ames and I were seeing each other for a few months before he had to serve three months in jail for violating his probation. While he was gone, we stayed in contact but I was still seeing other guys. At first, I didn't think us seeing each other would turn into a relationship. I had already experienced a man telling me how much he loved me while still having other females on the side. So when he told me he loved me in a letter from prison, I told him I loved him too but I really didn't take him seriously.

I met a guy by the name of Pinaro while James was away and we ended up sleeping together. But to my surprise, the more James and I talked and wrote letters to each other; the more I started falling for him. Once I realized James and I were getting serious, I stopped all contact with Pinaro. But little did I know, that would not be the last time I would hear from him or that our sleeping together would almost cost me my relationship with James.

I moved into a one-bedroom apartment after being evicted from the one I shared with my cousin and friend. Once James was released, he moved in and five months later, I became pregnant. During the first few months of my pregnancy, everyone made comments about my stomach being too big to just be pregnant with one baby. So it came as no surprise when I saw two heads appear on the ultrasound screen. I remember tears falling down my face and James asking me what was wrong. I really could not explain how I felt because I was full of mixed emotions; I was happy and afraid at the same time. James and I both had family history of twins. However, my mother's side had a history of the vanishing twin syndrome. I had a few family members who started out pregnant with twins but one twin wouldn't have a heartbeat, and the fetus eventually reabsorbed into the placenta. Therefore, I was automatically concerned if both babies would survive. Also having had an abortion in the past, I was unsure if that would cause any complications.

I was also very worried about how he and I were going to provide for two babies at once. I was now working as a front desk representative at the hotel only making ten dollars an hour. James was no longer working at the hotel due to him being in jail and his criminal background made it difficult for him to get another job. But we knew something had to happen quickly with twin baby girls on the way.

As the next several months went by, my belly became the size of a watermelon and I gained the amount of weight my doctor recommended and more. It was the beginning of the month of May and James's family was having a celebration for his mother's birthday. As I sat at the table eating, James tapped me and said he wanted me to meet his friend. We had talked about this guy he was close friends with while growing up and how they had a falling out a year before he and I started dating. When I looked up and saw Pinaro's face, to say I was shocked would be an understatement. James introduced him by a completely different name as he reached out to shake my hand. I extended my hand as we awkwardly greeted each other. He and James began to carry on a conversation as I sat there silently with embarrassment. I was so puzzled by this guy lying to me about his name. Then it turned out that he was in a relationship with James's god sister and they were planning to get married. I felt so bad and knew I had to tell him sooner than later.

When we returned home from the birthday celebration, I could not shake the anxiousness I felt about telling James that I slept with his friend over a year ago. Although I didn't know they were friends, I was still nervous about how he would react. As he sat down on the couch, I walked over to him and sat down on his lap as he rubbed my belly. Tears began to form in my eyes as I took a deep breath and began telling him that I knew the guy he introduced to me. I told him about meeting Pinaro while he was in prison and that we slept together. I could feel his body tense up as I went on telling him that his friend lied to me about his name. He removed me from his lap as his voice became louder with anger. As I repeatedly told him I was sorry, I could see the hurt in his eyes. I tried explaining to him that in the beginning I never took us talking seriously while he was in jail. However, once he was released, I started getting serious with him and had been faithful since. However, I knew there was nothing I could say to make the situation any better. He walked away from me and didn't speak to me for the rest of the night.

A couple days went by with us not speaking and I didn't like the cold shoulder he was giving me. I was thirty-five weeks and couldn't handle the level of stress I was having. I finally told him I needed him to talk to me. I needed to know how he felt and if he still wanted to be with me. He expressed that he still loved me and wanted to be with me. However, it would take him a while to get over what I had done. I knew it would take a while for him to forgive me but I was grateful that he was finally talking to me and loved me enough to stay.

On May 30th, 2008, I had a scheduled cesarean section due to both girls being breech. I was thirty-eight weeks when the girls arrived with Kevyona weighing 5 pounds 12 ounces and TeMariona weighing 6 pounds 7 ounces. Over the next three months, while on maternity leave and healing from the cesarean, we were having the hardest time making ends meet. James landed a job working at Target, but child support for his three other children cut most of his paychecks down. My paycheck was enough to cover the rent, but did not cover all of our basic needs. It was to the point that we had to pawn some of our things just to make ends meet. James applied to school to become a barber, but was denied financial aid due to the amount of child support he owed. After he applied to other schools with no success, we came to an agreement that it would be best for me to go back to school.

Medical assistant programs were very popular at the time. After sitting down with an advisor at Minneapolis Business College, I was informed that it would only take me nine months to complete the program, and would graduate with a diploma in Medical Assisting. James's sister-in-law had just graduated with a medical assisting degree and was already working making a nice amount of money. I never envisioned myself working in the medical field after being in hospitality for eight years. However, I was determined to better our lives the best and fastest way possible. I enrolled into college to receive my Medical Assistant Diploma and James agreed to stay at home with the girls. We did whatever we had to in order to make sure we ate each day and that I had bus money to get to school and work.

It was the wintertime and the weather was harsh, so getting on the bus with two 4-month-old babies in car seats was a bit of a challenge. One day while working at the front desk, I shared with a coworker about me starting school and that the only transportation I had was the bus. My coworker told me his parents were getting rid of a car and offered the vehicle to us. It was a very old two-door car with a piece of the floor in the car caved in, but I was grateful. There were times we had to pour water in it just for it to run, but it got us from one destination to the next and we didn't have to pay a dime for the vehicle.

Monday through Friday, I attended school during the day and went to work during the evenings. I came home after work and regularly woke up in the middle of the night to feed my precious girls. James continued to stay home with the girls due to childcare being so expensive. There were times I would call James on my way to school crying because I felt so bad leaving him to care for them alone. But he would remind me of why I was going to school and that it was to make a better life for us.

Working, going to school fulltime and taking care of the girls took so much energy out of me. I was no longer keeping up with cleaning our home, dirty clothes were piling up, and the apartment looked a mess. My body had changed after having the girls and I went from weighing 140-150 pounds to weighing over 200 pounds. I was no longer giving James a lot of attention in the bedroom. I was so focused on school, work, and being a mother that I forgot to be his lover. It was so much going on in our lives that I didn't even notice the signs of him slowly pulling away from me.

One day while I was at school, I received a phone call from the mother of James's older son and daughter. Over the past two and a half years of James and I being together, she and I had our exchange of not so pleasant words since she disrespected James on multiple occasions. Once I heard her voice on the other end of the phone, I was already on guard for whatever she had to say. She said she was calling to let me know that James had been calling her talking badly about me. She went on to say that she had been in my apartment on more than one occasion while I was not home. At first, I did not believe any of what she said until she started describing the inside of our apartment. She said she liked the Chinese decorations I had on our bathroom wall and how she saw my broken drawer on my dresser in our bedroom. I was furious, hurt, and felt disrespected all at the same time. There I was at school trying to make a better life for us and the man I was in love with and trusted with every bit of me had this woman in our home. After hanging up with her, I was distraught and believed every word that had come out of that woman's mouth.

When I confronted James about what she said to me, he said she was lying and she had never been in our home. But I knew better. How else would this woman know what the inside of my home looked like? I didn't believe him and from that point on, I started to lose trust in him.

After a little over nine months of challenging and demanding work, I graduated with my Diploma in Medical Assisting and was hired through a medical assisting temp agency making fourteen dollars an hour. I was able to let go of my job at the hotel and work full time for the agency. A lot had happened that year, James and I even had our three-year anniversary of being together. He proposed to me and although I still had a trust issue, I said yes. We moved into a nice two-bedroom duplex, bought a 2003 Chevrolet Impala and James had a studio setup in our basement for recording music. It felt good to see things were finally looking up for us. Our daughters were a little over one-years-old and James was still staying at home with them. He had gotten tired of not working and started selling marijuana. I was never okay with him selling marijuana. However, I could not stop him from doing what he felt was the only way he could provide for us at the time.

Several months after moving into the duplex, I received a phone call from James while I was at work. He asked me if the owner of the home had informed me of an electric company coming to install wiring in the house. I thought it was a bit weird because the owner and I were always communicating and he never mentioned needing to have anything installed in the home. Because my name was on the lease and James's name was not, he did not let them into the home. Then one week later, a stranger knocked on the door and asked if he could buy marijuana from me. I could not believe what he had just asked me! I told him he had the wrong house and slammed the door in his face! I told James that these two events were very weird and that he needed to stop selling marijuana out of our home. Well it is said that warning comes before destruction. Little did I know; our lives were about to change for the worst.

It was about a week later when I was speaking to James over the phone while at work. Christmas was a few days away, so he told me that he and a friend were about to go Christmas shopping. He said the girls were with his cousin and that he was going to pick them up once they were done shopping. Later that day, I pulled up to our home after work and noticed a red truck I had not seen before parked in my usual spot. I figured our neighbor that lived above us must have had company over. As I walked up to the front door of our home, I put my key inside of the lock. Before I could open the door, I was met by a police officer opening my door for me.

The police officer asked, "Are you Ms. Jarrett?" I replied, "Yes" and he then asked me to have a seat in a chair in the kitchen area. As I sat down, I saw James and his friend both sitting at our dining room table in handcuffs. There were two other officers in the dining room in civilian clothing with their badges exposed. I looked over to James as he shook his head in disbelief. That is when I noticed a big zip lock bag of marijuana on the dining room table. The officer who had opened the door began to tell me that they had been watching our home for the past couple of months and noticed traffic coming and going from our house. He also mentioned one of our neighbors complained of "suspicious activity" coming from our home. He stated that they knew this was a family home and had seen me leaving and coming home from work. So instead of them busting through our windows, putting guns in our faces, they came to our home for what they call a "knock and talk". He stated once James opened the door, they could smell marijuana coming from the inside and that gave them probable cause to enter our home. They had no warrant at the time; however, they held us in our home due to probable cause until they obtained a warrant to search the home. About two hours later, they had a warrant and ripped the house apart completely searching for other drugs and/or weapons.

I knew there was a gun in our home because James had taken the gun from his younger cousin. A few weeks prior, his cousin got into an altercation with someone and pulled the gun out on that person. James took the gun away from him and brought it to our home temporarily. After searching and searching, they located ecstasy pills, bottles of promethazine and the gun. Since James was currently on probation for a previous gun charge, they arrested him immediately. I was informed that I had 72 hours to have all of our things moved out due to drugs being in the home. As I was handed a copy of the police report, I stood there in disbelief of what had just taken place. In that moment, my fiancé and his friend were being led out of our home in hand cuffs, arrested for drugs and weapon possession and we had just lost our home. The only good thing about this situation was that our daughters were still with James's cousin and not at home during all the chaos. She had told him that they were asleep so he decided to wait on picking them up. If they had been present at the time of the police search, they probably would have tried to take my daughters away.

The next day I received a call from the landlord. He told me he was contacted by the police and was informed he had to evict me out of the home. He told me that although we were supposed to be off the property within seventy-two hours, he would give me until after Christmas. Christmas was in three days and he would feel bad having us move out on Christmas Day. I was so grateful, but I couldn't think straight for the life of me. I was worried about James. I had not heard from him since he was arrested and I had four days to find a place to move. I curled up in my bed and cried until I couldn't cry anymore. My sister Rochelle didn't stay far from where we lived, so she came over. I told her about everything that happened as I sat on my bed smoking a black and mild cigar trying to figure out our next move. She helped me clean up because I hadn't picked up anything since the police tossed our belongings all over the house. I called James's cousin and after telling her about everything that happened, she offered to keep the girls overnight so that I could work on putting the house back together.

I finally received a call from James the next day. He had already informed his family about what happened. He and his dad were already in the process of trying to post bail. They called my uncle who could contact a lawyer to help get him released. James told him everything that happened and my uncle obtained a lawyer to speak on James's behalf. The lawyer got him released the same day on bail and back home in time to celebrate Christmas with us.

I was so happy that James was home and that the girls had a great Christmas but I was hurting inside. There was still so much pending. We had been in contact with James's brother's landlord regarding a home he had for rent. We were approved for the home and had twenty-four hours left to move out of the home. At the same time, we were also waiting for James's court date regarding his sentencing. We were fighting the case due to the police not having a warrant to enter our home from the beginning. I was not home at the time and James said he did not give them permission to come into our home. He stated the officers forced their way in and that was when they saw the bag of marijuana on the table. The lawyer who helped James post bail stated we had a big chance of winning and was willing to take on his case; however, he wanted three thousand dollars up front. But after Christmas and moving, we just did not have that amount of money to pay him.

The house we moved into was "a hole in the wall" with a mouse problem. I would hear mice in the middle of the night and see their droppings in the kitchen. I was constantly telling the landlord about it, but the problem was never resolved. I couldn't take dealing with it especially with the risk of one of my daughters being harmed. Although we signed a 6- month lease, I had already started looking for another house for us to move into.

We were still trying to gather the money to hire the lawyer in hopes that James may not have to serve time at all. I was still working for the staffing agency at the time, but I was offered a fulltime position working at a clinic in Minneapolis. Although we lived in Saint Paul, I took the position as an opportunity to get my foot in the door and potentially transfer to a clinic in Saint Paul. The clinic was nice but the pay was nicer and it couldn't have come at a better time. I was making more money, which meant we might have the money to pay for the lawyer we needed in no time. Not to mention James and his brothers were starting to perform in nightclubs opening for music artists. Their performances would keep James out throughout the night, at times not coming home until the next morning. He would call and tell me he was spending the night at a friend's or his brother's house because he was too intoxicated to drive.

One morning I had gotten up before James. He was still passed out from the night after being drunk and out all night. I had never felt the need to go through James's phone before, but something was tugging me to do it. I walked over to his side of the bed and pulled his phone out of his pocket. I went into our bathroom and started looking at his text messages. The last message that was received was from a woman whose name I did not recognize. I didn't know a family member or friend of his by that name so I opened the messages. As I read the text messages my stomach dropped. The messages clearly showed they were in an intimate relationship and one message even mentioned him having a key to this woman's home. I could not believe what I was reading.

We had been together for close to four years and he had proposed to me almost a year ago. Just when I thought things were going to be okay with us, I was wrong. The messages dated all the way back to six months before, and he had gotten a new phone between that time so who knows how long they had actually been seeing each other. I just had to speak with her and find out just how long their fling had been going on.

My nerves were shot as I pressed call on James's phone and heard this woman's voice on the other end. But I knew I had to get myself together, I didn't want to curse her out or threaten to beat her down. We were grown women and if I wanted her to tell me anything, I needed to approach her as a woman. I introduced myself to her telling her I was James's "wife" and the mother of his twin daughters. Although we were not married yet, we had been together long enough and I wanted her to know where I stood with him. She immediately told me she knew about me but did not know James and I were together. She said he told her that we were friends but were no longer in a relationship. She said they had been seeing each other for almost a year. She also mentioned she had attended James's performance the night before and he came to her house after. She went on to apologize but I just couldn't take it anymore. I told her she could have him and that she could help him come up with the three thousand he needed to stay out of jail. I was in tears after hanging up with her. I just didn't know what to make of it, so I started asking myself what I had done wrong that made him go astray. It felt as if my mind was going a mile a minute trying to understand what I had just discovered. I even began to wonder if it was revenge because I slept with Pinaro.

I was beating myself up about something that happened nearly five years prior; but I just didn't understand why else James would cheat on me. I was all over the place and just could not think straight. I went for a walk to the store and bought a pack of Black and Mild Cigars, which had become my best friend since the raid. The chaos was too much for me to handle. When I walked into the house, James was awake and I had to refrain myself from running up to him and slapping his cheating behind. It took me a little while to confront him but he knew something was wrong with me.

I sat on the edge of our bed smoking the cigar as he got dressed and asked me if I was okay. It was then that I asked him about this mystery woman. At first, he acted as if he didn't know who she was until I told him I had spoken to her after reading their text messages. Then, he became silent. My nerves were so bad; I can truly say I know what it feels like before a woman commits murder because I sat there on the edge of the bed ready to kill him. I just needed him to say something, but he kept silent. In that moment, I lost it, I cried my eyes out asking him what was wrong with me. I asked him what I did that led him to cheat on me. I needed him to tell me what was wrong in our relationship because I thought it was my fault. I asked him if this was his way of getting back at me for sleeping with his friend years ago. I just didn't understand and I needed answers. In the midst of my tears, he told me I did nothing to make him cheat. He said he was seeing the other woman because she was going to help pay for the lawyer that we needed to beat his case. He said he didn't love her, that he loved me. He didn't want to lose his family but she was willing to give him the money.

I was so naïve that it made sense to me and I agreed for him to continue seeing her just to get the money. Yes, I know I was delusional. What woman in her right mind would agree for the love of her life to see another woman to get money? But the problem was, I wasn't in my right mind.

After a few days of thinking about what I had just approved for him to do, I expressed to him that I couldn't allow him to do it. I told him we could get the money another way but I could not take him seeing another woman. He agreed to break things off with her and understood how I felt. A few months went by and I would find myself constantly searching through his phone to see if he was keeping in contact with her. I even started checking his inbox messages on Facebook and found that he was not only still seeing the woman he cheated on me with, but was messaging other women as well. From then on, our relationship was like a domino effect. I would continuously argue with him no matter where we were. If I felt he looked at another woman the wrong way, I would fight with him. One fight got so bad while I was intoxicated, that I pulled a knife out on him and the police had to be called to our home. In that moment, I saw myself as my mother.

When I was younger, there were many nights I would hear my mother and her ex-husband fighting and the police being called to the house. I promised myself I would never be in a relationship like theirs. Nevertheless, there I was drunk and fighting this man that I loved so much, and saw myself being with for the rest of my life. However, I was hurting and I didn't know how to properly express the pain I was feeling inside. I had to make a decision. I had to decide if I was going to forgive him and move on, or be done with the relationship completely. After that night, I decided that I would stick by his side as we awaited his sentencing, but after that, I was done.

A few months later, we were moving again, I was at home with the girls pulling boxes into the kitchen to put on the moving truck when I heard a noise coming from the room where James had his studio equipment. Next thing I knew, there was a guy running out of the room. He climbed through the window and before I could make a move, he opened the back door. Suddenly five or six people rushed into our house and started taking the studio equipment. I was in panic mode; I recognized one of the guys and knew he had been in our house before. I reached for my phone to try to call James but the guy I recognized began walking towards me. He knocked the phone out of my hand and put his hand under his shirt as if he was holding a gun underneath. Just then, I heard my daughters crying behind me. I told him to take whatever they wanted. They were taking our things and ran out of the back door as I grabbed my daughters and ran out of the front door.

I drove to James's mother's house in tears and shaken up from the robbery. When we got there, I called James. I explained to him everything that had just happened and that I recognized one of the guys. I believed the guy might have come over our house before to do some music recording in his studio. By the time James and his brothers made it to the house, the guys were gone. They had taken all the studio equipment and our flat screen televisions. Although I wanted them to find the guys that had come into our home, I didn't want James getting involved since he was already dealing with other charges. We continued to pack up our things and moved out the next day.

We spent the next 365 days walking on eggs shells. We just didn't know when James was going to be sentenced since his sentencing date was pushed back multiple times. Then January of 2012, James was sentenced to five years in prison. He was initially facing up to 15 years in prison, but thankfully, the judge dropped the drug charges that were against him and charged him with a parole violation with possession of a weapon. As he was taken away in handcuffs from the courtroom, I nearly lost it. Seeing him leaving with the officers and knowing he was not coming back out took a toll on me.

The first couple of months of James's absence was hard for me to process and took a toll on our daughters. Their three-year-old minds did not understand why their father was not home anymore. They went from being with him 100% of the time to seeing him once or twice a month. They started missing him so much that I would find them crying in their beds and it hurt so bad to see them crying for him. I had to put my emotions aside to be there for them physically and emotionally.

I can finally admit that I went through a period of

depression. I lost between fifteen to twenty pounds. I would get drunk at home and smoke cigars. I was getting into arguments with James over the phone because I had so much anger and bitterness towards him. I felt like I was carrying a ton bricks on my shoulders while trying to keep up with the bills on my own. One part of me was trying to be supportive for him mentally, emotionally and financially while being all those things for our daughters as well. At the same time, I was ready to give up on our nearly six year relationship. I had so many emotions bottled up inside; I felt alone and had no one to lean on for support. After James had been in prison for three months, I decided to end things. I knew it was not going to be easy; however, I was done with putting my feelings aside. It was time to start thinking about what was best for me.

I continued to be as supportive as I could be while getting to a place of focusing on what was best for my daughters and me. The raid, the cheating, the robbery and James no longer being with us were life-altering situations. I was now a single mother and I desired to provide my daughters with a better life. I believe James going to prison was a way of separating me from a relationship that was unhealthy for me. Prior to our relationship, I was still unsure of who I was and where I was going in life. I had become a fiancée to James, a mother to my twin daughters, and nothing to myself. I had no idea of who I was. I was raising little girls that were watching my every move. I had a tremendous responsibility of raising them in the right way.

But the first thing I had to do was figure out who I was.

# Chapter 6

# Rude Awakening

*I*t had been a couple months since James was sentenced to prison and I was a mess emotionally. But at the same time relieved for ending our engagement because I knew I deserved better. I'd thrown myself a "bachelorette" themed birthday party in celebration of not being engaged anymore. I viewed myself as a bachelorette with no ring and felt free to do whatever I wanted to do.

I was slowly going back to the old partying lifestyle I had prior to meeting James and becoming a mother. I even reached out to a few guys from my past. One was a guy that I had known since high school. We started talking over the phone and eventually he invited me over to his house. We would hang out from time to time, and then one day we slept together. It was a mistake because he was not someone I could see myself being in a relationship with. I never viewed him the same and eventually stopped all contact with him. But I had this continuing void in my heart that I was trying to fill some way or another. If it wasn't going out to a nightclub, it was drinking and smoking. I was back to watching pornography and eventually reached out to another guy friend.

This guy had always shown interest in me in the past,

but I just could not bring myself to want him as more than a friend. He was one of the first people to be there for me and my daughters after James had gone to prison. We would sit on my porch and just talk until the wee hours of the morning. He never tried to have sex with me. He offered his ears to hear my frustrations and even cuddled with me while sleeping over his house. I knew he wanted more and I felt bad for dragging him along, knowing things would not go any further. I knew I needed to bring an end to the way things were going because I did not want to continue leading him on. At the same time, I felt like I needed him because I was broken. However, nothing I did, not marijuana, alcohol or sex could fix the brokenness I felt.

During this time, I had been in contact with my cousin, who I will call Naomi. She was also Tiffany's sister. She and I were very close when we were much younger, but we eventually went our separate ways as we got older. She was a member of a church I had visited a few times in the past, and invited me to come to church with her one Sunday morning. I went with her that Sunday and from then on, I started attending church more often. However, there were a few Sundays I wouldn't make it because of a hangover from partying the night before.

One weekend I had gone out to a nightclub with Tiffany and Kay. It was her birthday weekend, so we went out to a lounge in Minneapolis to celebrate. It was the middle of June and the weather was perfect. We were drinking before we headed out. I was in such a good mood and feeling the alcohol before we got to the lounge. As we walked from the parking ramp where I parked my car, we began taking pictures and having a good time. Once we entered the lounge, Tiffany and Kay immediately made their way to the dance floor. However, I wasn't in the mood to dance and suddenly I felt as if I was not supposed to be there. Kay noticed me sitting down and tried to get me to come on the dance floor, but I waved her off and told her I was fine. I sat most of the time, didn't have much to drink, and was ready to leave.

As the lounge was closing and we were heading out of the building, Tiffany went back into the lounge because she thought she lost her phone. As she went in, something came over me and I started crying uncontrollably. Kay, thinking James was the source of my tears, walked up to me and started talking to me about him. But I walked away from her out of frustration because I knew I was not crying because of him. I could not stop crying and tears were flooding out of my eyes as I continued walking downtown Minneapolis. I had no idea why I was crying and nothing significant had triggered it. I completely left my cousin and friend, made my way to the parking ramp where my Chevrolet Impala was parked, and drove to my home in Saint Paul. Shortly after I made it home, Tiffany and Kay were knocking on the door. They ended up getting a ride with someone they knew from the lounge and stopped by to make sure I made it home. From the moment they left, my life began to change. It was the night, God later revealed to me, that He had forgiven me for every sin I had committed and through my crying, He was cleansing me.

Two Sundays later, I attended church with Naomi. After the Bishop finished altar call, they had already started baptism and church service was ending. I sat waiting for Naomi as she fellowshipped with other members of the church, when suddenly; I had the desire to be baptized. I had received baptism with my mom and siblings when I was younger, however, once I started attending church again I decided I wanted to be baptized again. I had planned for my daughters to be baptized with me the following year on their birthday; however, God had a different plan.

I asked Naomi if they were still conducting baptisms. She said yes and directed me to a person that could help me with paperwork and prepare for baptism. As I walked down the hallway to the office, everything felt so surreal. I filled out the paperwork and I was given items to change into.

There were two men standing on both sides of me to help me as I walked down the steps into the pool of water. I remember one asking me if I believed in Jesus Christ. He asked if I believed Jesus Christ died for my sins, rose again on the third day and asked if I accepted Jesus Christ as my Lord and Savior. When I said yes, they baptized me in the name of Jesus, lowered my body under the water and brought me back up. The old "me" died in that water, the one who didn't know who she was and was trying to fill voids within her heart with other resources because she didn't know that God was The Source. A new me had come out of that water and was raised in Christ Jesus. As I rose from the water, I saw my daughters who were four years-old at the time cheering me on saying, "Yay mommy!" Naomi and her sister were there with them clapping and cheering me on, as I cried while the men helped me up the steps of the pool.

I felt as if I was walking on clouds as I went to the bathroom to change back into my clothes. When I got into the bathroom, I laid down on the floor, crying tears of pure joy. Someone had to come and call me out of the bathroom because my family was looking for me. When I was finally able to change out of the wet clothing, I came out and walked back into the sanctuary. My daughters ran up to me, hugging me, as some of the church members congratulated me.

God called me that day although I had already been baptized as a child. When I was a child, I did not understand the meaning of baptism, how it was a symbol of being born again as a new person. I was no longer a child, but this time getting baptized as an adult. There was an unknown transformation beginning within me. In that very moment at the age of twenty-seven, God called me back to Him and I was born again.

Although, my situation hadn't changed, I had a whole new perspective. I now had a sense of hope that assured me that my daughters and I were going to be fine. Prior to James going to prison, he was still staying home with our daughters while I went to work. Once the girls turned four years old, they were approved to attend a Head Start program that was close to our home in Saint Paul. The program was wonderful and the hours were convenient for my work schedule. I could drop them off as I headed for work and pick them up after work. It took some time for the girls to get accustomed to being away from their dad and me. During the first week, they would cry their little eyes out and did not want me to leave. But one of the teachers turned out to be James's aunt, which eventually made the girls feel comfortable. Things were slowly looking up for us. We were attending church consistently and had developed a church family of women and men that embraced my daughters and me with open arms.

I gave my landlord a thirty-day notice for us to move out of the house. I knew I could no longer afford it on my own and needed to downsize until I was at a comfortable place financially. It was Friday, July 13, 2012 and I was driving home from a church event with my daughters, Naomi, and her daughter in the car. Naomi and I were laughing about a song we heard on the radio. As I laughed, I did not hear Naomi utter the words "They're not stopping," I then heard her yell, "Mika, they're really not stopping!" As I turned to look, it was too late. All I could do was turn around to the back seat and look at the three little girls that had no idea of what was about to happen, as I braced myself for the impact. The car hit us and all I heard were voices screaming. After the impact, my heart was beating fast as I looked in the back seat to see if my daughters and Naomi's daughter were okay. Thankfully, they were fine, but were startled and crying because of the impact.

However, Naomi was screaming at the top of her lungs. I was afraid to look over at her because the car hit her passenger door. The driver who had just t-boned my car, while running a red light, didn't even get out of the car to make sure we were alright. As I unbuckled my seatbelt to get out of the car, the driver reversed their car and sped off! I was in complete shock, but knew I had to check on Naomi. As I rushed over to the passenger side door, it was completely smashed in. Naomi's screaming frightened me because I didn't know what condition she was in. People started running into the street toward us. Voices were yelling saying they called the police and were asking if we were okay. I got my daughters and Naomi's daughter out of the car. When the paramedics came, they took Naomi out and put her in the back of an ambulance to examine her for injuries. When the police arrived, I was still in shock from the impact as an officer asked me if I could describe the car that hit us. I only knew the color of the car, but there were witnesses who could give a better description.

I was relieved to hear Naomi was fine but had slight pain from the impact. Then reality set in. I realized my car was completely wrecked with the entire right side smashed, oil leaking and not drivable. My car insurance had expired and I had not renewed it. They were not able to find the hit and run driver, my car was a lost cause and had to be towed from the scene. I called James's mom and told her what happened. She and her husband immediately came to the scene and gave us a ride home.

Having no vehicle made things very difficult for me. My daughters and I would get up very early in the morning and take the city bus to Head Start. From there, I had to ride the bus to Minneapolis for work. I was arriving to work ten to fifteen minutes late due to the bus stop being several blocks away from the clinic. After a couple weeks of being tardy, my supervisor had a meeting with me. She had been keeping track of my tardiness and was concerned. I told her about the car accident and that riding the bus was causing me to be late. She said she understood but forewarned me that if my tardiness continued, she would have to give me a written warning. I was relieved that it was only a verbal warning; but now I was worried about losing my job.

That very same day, one of my coworkers approached me because she had heard about my car accident. She stayed near my home and offered to let me carpool with her to work. To this day, I realize that she was my saving grace. She would not only pick me up and drop me off, but she offered to drop my daughters off as we headed for work. In the meantime, I was applying for a position I could transfer to that was in Saint Paul. I had also applied for a car loan and after having an interview for the loan, I was certain I would be approved.

I remember it like it was yesterday. It was mid-August of 2012 and I was sitting in the bathroom tub crying because I had just received the decision for my car loan. I was extremely hurt as I read the denial letter. Just as things seemed to start working out for us, I was being pulled down again. That same month, my lease was up on the house and I hadn't found a place for us to move. I was feeling sorry for myself as I held a beer in one hand and a cigar in the other. The girls were sleeping and I was alone with my thoughts. It was about three o clock in the morning when I finally got out of the bathtub. I walked over to my laptop, opened a document and began typing about my life. Around six in the morning and twelve pages later, I closed my laptop and went to bed.

The next day while talking to James on the phone, he said he mentioned to his mother that the girls and I needed a place to stay. She agreed to let us stay for a year with no hesitation, which would allow me to save up enough money for a vehicle. I was so relieved and grateful that she would welcome us into her home although James and I were no longer together. As the end of the month approached, I decided not to keep some of my furniture. I placed my table and chair set near the curb and taped a "for free" sign on it. By the time I came back outside to put something else on the curb, I noticed the table set was already gone. I went back into the house and grabbed a few other items, when I noticed James's mom pulling up to the house. She came to help me with any items I would be bringing to their house. She helped me put the other items on the curb when I saw a woman carrying the other items I had just brought out of the house to another house across the street. So, we decided to walk the rest of the items to her. As we walked up to her home, we noticed she was having a yard sale. The woman had placed all the items I had on the curb in her yard to be a part of her yard sale. We handed her the rest of what we had as she smiled and thanked us. I was just grateful to see that what I was letting go of could be of use to someone else.

I took my bed and our clothing to James's mother's house and everything else went to storage. She and her husband owned a three bedroom home. They slept in the master while my daughters and I used the other two bedrooms. Moving in with them, I felt a sense of peace and knowing that she was a believer in Christ gave me more assurance that we were in good hands. She had a room in her home full of statues with Jesus in the manger along with paintings and crosses that all represented Christ. At times, I would go in that room just to have peace of mind. I was unsure of many things in my life. I had no vehicle, no house, and my job was in jeopardy from being tardy on the days my coworker was not able to pick us up. I desired change and just didn't know where to start.

A couple months later, both of my daughters became sick at the same time. They both were running a fever, but I kept it under control with Tylenol. In the middle of the night, TeMari woke up out of her sleep screaming and when I picked her up, she was very hot. When I checked her temperature, it was 104.3, which was the highest fever either of them had ever had. I was in panic mode asking James's mom if we should call the ambulance. However, she said it wasn't necessary and suggested I take her to an emergency room. I was still in a panic as I rushed about getting my daughters together. Since working in the medical field, I learned that a high fever in children could cause a seizure. I was trying to stay calm for their sake, but I was falling apart on the inside.

As I drove to an emergency room, I glanced at Kevy who was not feeling good at all but TeMari was smiling and talking, although she had the highest fever! As we walked into the emergency room, we were checked in right away. It was busy, so I expected there would be a long wait to be called back to a room. Patiently, I sat down with the girls in front of the television. But about ten minutes later, their names were called to have their vitals taken. When Temari's temperature was checked, it had gone down from 104.3 to 98.2 and I was shocked because of how quickly her fever went down!

The nurse told me it may be a long wait due to there being nine other people in front of us and said we could go back to our seats. But not even 30 minutes later, we were being called back. The nurse took us to a room and asked a few questions. She did a nasal sample from the girls for influenza testing and told me that the doctor would be in shortly. The girls laid on the bed as they watched cartoons on the television in the exam room. It was past midnight and I was scheduled to work that morning but I was exhausted and worried about what was going on with my babies. As I waited, the telephone in the room began to ring. I just ignored it because I figured they were calling the wrong number. After several rings, it finally stopped. Then a couple minutes later, it was ringing again. I got up to look at the caller ID but there was no name and it displayed a number that was unfamiliar to me. Again, I just let it ring until the person hung up. But the phone rang again. I let it ring several times until I finally decided to answer it. As I said "Hello," the woman on the other end of the phone said, "Hi, I'm looking for my son." I explained to her that she must have had the wrong number and that she was calling a phone located in an emergency exam room. She said, "Oh, okay." Then she suddenly said to me, "Everything will be alright, so don't worry because God is with you." Tears ran down my face as I said thank you and hung up the phone. I could not believe what she had just said to me, but I knew my daughters were going to be alright.

Shortly after the phone encounter, the doctor walked in and said their nasal smear came back positive for Influenza. They were prescribed antibiotics and I was instructed to keep the girls home for a couple days to prevent them from spreading it to others. It was around one o'clock Monday morning as we left the emergency room. I was so relieved to finally know what was going on with my daughters, but I hated the fact I would have to call into work for the next two days. My supervisor was already on my case about being tardy; and I just didn't want to give her any other reason to write me up. When I returned to work, my supervisor called me into her office. I explained to her that my daughters were diagnosed with the flu and how I had to be home to care for them. She went on to ask about their father, which led me to open up to her about him being in prison. I explained to her that I didn't have many family members or friends that I could ask to keep the girls because they had to work as well. She informed me that she was giving me a written warning. However, if I missed too many days, I would receive another written warning. She told me that she understood and asked if there was anything she could do to help. I assured her that we were fine and that my daughters were feeling better.

Over the next couple of months, Head Start was closed for teacher conference, which caused me to miss work a few more days. This time, my supervisor called me into her office again to talk about the missed days and issued another written warning and I knew I could lose my job. One of my coworkers mentioned that she had also been written up a couple times for being just a few minutes tardy and felt our manager was intentionally singling us out. She began to have her meetings with a union representative present to speak for her and recommended that I do the same. She gave me the contact information for a woman who not only worked the urgent care shift in the clinic but was also a union representative. I spoke with her regarding my situation since I could potentially lose my job if I called out again. She understood my situation, helped me to understand my rights as an employee covered under the union and assured me that she would be available for me if I was called into my manager's office again. Two months later after feeling as if I could lose my job any day, a nurse manager contacted me regarding the position I applied for a couple months before. The job was in Saint Paul and was ten minutes away from where we lived. She wanted to do a phone interview with me regarding the position. After the phone interview, she scheduled me for an in-person interview with the clinic manager that following week. Once I completed the interview, I was offered the position. This job offer came just in time and it was a much easier commute on the bus line. I proudly put in my two-week notice because I no longer had to worry about being called into my supervisor's office for my attendance.

A couple weeks later, I was so relieved to be walking into the doors of my new job. As I started shadowing a Certified Medical Assistant, she informed me of the clinic's workflow. There was five providers seeing at least eighty patients daily. There were also different specialties within the department such as, Medical Spine, Neurology, and Physical Medicine Rehabilitation. However, all five providers shared four exam rooms. Each provider had their own paperwork and their own color system so that each provider would know which room their patient was located in. At first, I just didn't understand how it was possible to keep each provider on time for their patients with only four exam rooms to work out of. Not to mention the different specialties for each one and having to keep up with their assorted colors. This seemed impossible for me and I could feel myself getting discouraged. I felt so overwhelmed thinking that the job was not right or me. I informed the Certified Medical Assistant that I needed to step away to go to the bathroom.

As I closed the door behind me, I leaned against the bathroom door saying, "Lord, I can't handle this position" and went on praying about how the job was too overwhelming. After I finished venting to the Lord, I took a deep breath and walked back to the nurses' station. The Certified Medical Assistant I had been following said to me, "Are you ready to room your first patient?" I reluctantly said "sure." She said, "Ok, your first patient's name is Jesus." I looked at her in disbelief and stared at the paper just to be sure I heard her correctly. I asked if she was sure the patient's name was pronounced the same as Jesus or if it was pronounced as "Hesus" but she said, "No, he pronounces it as Jesus." I was in complete shock because it was the first time I had ever met someone whose name was spelled Jesus and actually pronounced it as Jesus. Just after venting to God, I did not believe that the name of the first patient that I was rooming being Jesus was a coincidence. I believed that it was the Lord's way of speaking to me, reminding me that He was with me and that this position was for me. From that moment on, the job was not as difficult as I thought and I caught on very easily.

I still did not have a vehicle, but with my new job location being in Saint Paul, it was much more convenient than taking the bus to Minneapolis. One day after church, a friend told me about a car dealership in Brooklyn Park. She had just gotten her new vehicle and told me that they were flexible with allowing you to put a minimum of two hundred dollars down on the vehicle of your choice. So, I went on the website to see what vehicles they had to offer. I wasn't interested in any of the vehicles until I came across a white truck. I called the dealership and asked if it was still available. But the gentleman on the other line told me the truck would not be ready to be leased for at least another two weeks. I was a bit disappointed but I scheduled an appointment anyway to meet with a leasing agent that Saturday.

When the weekend arrived, my cousin, who I'll refer to as Andrea, drove me to the dealership. My sister Rochelle came along to apply for a vehicle as well. We met with two leasing agents and filled out the application. As I filled out the paperwork, the agent I was working with mentioned that she and I shared the same birthday. I took a mental note of this because I was noticing that the people God would bring into my life all had some type of connection with me. This assured me that I was in the right place at the right time for what God was doing. I asked the agent if she could tell me the status of the white truck that I saw online, hoping she would tell me it was ready. She said she would check into it and told us we could look around at the other vehicles as we waited for our applications to be processed. As we looked around, I still hadn't found any other car within my price range that I was interested in leasing. When we walked back into the building, she told me my application was approved.

Suddenly out of the corner of my eye, I saw the white truck being pulled up near the door. She looked at me with a smile and said, "If you want it, the truck is yours." There I was in tears because I wanted the truck so badly. I put two hundred dollars down and she told me I needed insurance on the truck before I could drive it off the lot. As we reviewed the car insurance quotes, I knew I didn't have enough money for it. Rochelle's application was denied, but she just so happened to have the amount of money with her I needed to get the insurance. Therefore, she let me borrow the money from her. When I was handed the keys to my new truck, I literally cried on the dealership floor. After a car accident and several months of my daughters and I taking the city bus, on December 21, 2012, I was driving off the car lot with a white 2003 Chevrolet Trailblazer!

The New Year was approaching and we had gone through so much in the past several months. I had lost close to ten pounds due to stress after the car accident; having to move out of our home and not to mention the difficulty I faced at my previous job. Finally, things were starting to fall into place for us. I had a new position I loved that was very close to where we were living. We had a new truck and God was working on me from the inside out. He had given me a second chance and had given me a new beginning.

From that day forward, I was never the same and I was transforming right before my own eyes. God was replacing my desires with His desires and I was being transformed in every area of my life. I had no desire to drink or smoke as much, and it eventually became non-existent. God was maturing me rapidly, it was as if my eyes were opened and I was starting to view things differently. I had a burning desire within me to know more about God and to grow in His Word. So, I started attending new member classes at church and one of the classes was about speaking in tongues. One of the teachers stated that speaking in tongues gave you the ability to speak directly to God. But I had no idea this class was preparing me for a divine encounter I would have with a patient that would enable me to receive the gift of speaking in tongues.

One of the providers I worked with at the clinic would personally give paperwork to her patients after their visit. This was something she liked to do for her patients as she walked them out of the exam room. But this time, she asked me to give her patient the paperwork, which I thought was kind of odd. When I walked into the exam room, I noticed the patient was in a wheelchair and was paraplegic from the waist down. I greeted her and read over her paperwork with her. When I was finished, I handed the patient the paperwork and began to reach for the door when I heard her start to cry. My heart went out to her as I turned around and started consoling her by rubbing her back. I didn't know what was wrong, so I began encouraging her by letting her know that everything would be alright. She began to speak; however, her speech was slurred which made it hard for me to understand what she was saying. She reached inside of her purse and as she pulled out a note pad, I noticed that she had a bible in her purse.

She opened the note pad and started writing. As she wrote, I began reading what she was having a tough time saying. She wrote down three things: "Thank you for the sunshine;" "Thank you for Maureen playing the guitar for us;" and the last thing she wrote was "These are my prayer requests." At first, I didn't know what to say because I had never experienced anything like this before. Then I began to understand and believed she needed me to pray to God regarding those prayers on her behalf.

That same day after work, I went home and went into prayer. I said, "God, I have some prayer requests for you." I asked Him for the ability to speak in tongues so that He would get the prayer requests directly just like my new members' teacher said. I remembered her saying how at first, it would sound like baby talk but she said to continue speaking anyway. As I fixed my lips to form words I had never spoken, it was as if I no longer had control over my lips. I had no idea of what I was saying as slob, snot, and tears ran down my face. When I finally stopped, I just laid there in my bed in awe. In that moment, I had peace in knowing God had received those prayer requests.

God was growing me spiritually; at times, I would find myself crying because of His goodness. I couldn't believe I had gone most of my life without really knowing Him. God was showing He wanted to use me and was developing some things in me to get me to the level He needed me to be. Even if it meant taking some things away to get me to fully depend on Him so that He could get the glory in my life.

# Chapter 7

# The Power of Agreement

*B*efore we moved in with James's mother, I had been considering moving out of state. There were a few people I knew from high school who had relocated to Texas and had been there for years. I had been in contact with a coworker that had recently moved from Minnesota to Dallas, Texas and she loved it. During this time, my cousin Naomi had moved in with her sister Tiffany and had been considering moving to another state as well. She told me she was planning on visiting North Carolina and asked if I wanted to come. There were members from the church we attended who had relocated to North Carolina, and heard nothing but great things from them about the state. She had been researching the state and how it was ranked as one of the best places to raise a family. I didn't know anything about North Carolina but agreed to join her for the trip.

In January 2013, we arrived in Raleigh, North Carolina. I had initially gone just to get a feel for the state and to see if I would be interested in moving with her as well. But as we were landing, I was pretty much ready to move when I noticed that the trees were still green with no snow in the middle of winter verses all the snow we had in Minnesota. North Carolina was so pretty and refreshing. I immediately took a liking to the tall and skinny pine trees that were everywhere we went. During our visit, we stayed in a hotel in Raleigh but found ourselves commuting to Durham a lot. We visited a few historically black universities during our stay and the people were so friendly. Once we returned to Minnesota, I informed Naomi that I was considering moving to North Carolina with her.

Once I had come back from visiting North Carolina, I started praying for God to show me if moving to North Carolina was a part of the plan He had for my life. Once I prayed that prayer, Naomi and I started coming together in prayer and fasting. We needed God to know that we were looking for Him to move on our behalf and open every door for us. Naomi was a Certified Medical Assistant as well, so we started searching for employment within the medical field. We applied to private clinics and even hospitals to no avail. Until one day while searching the Internet for jobs, I looked to see if there was an Interim Healthcare Staffing agency location in North Carolina. I worked for Interim in Minnesota when I first graduated and I found that there were two Interim locations in North Carolina. I was surprised to see that one of the locations was in Durham, North Carolina. I was reminded that we were in Durham for most of our visit. So, with Interim Healthcare Staffing being in Durham, it would be a wonderful place to start. After speaking with a woman from Interim, Naomi and I were informed that two positions were available for Medical Assistants. She told us that the assignments we would receive were within Duke

Hospital and Clinics. However, we would need to come to North Carolina to meet with her in June and do testing to see if we were a fit for the positions. If we met all of the criteria, we would be able to start working by July. In the meantime, we continued to research schools for the girls, places to live, and just continued to trust God through the process. I realized that although things were working in our favor, the more I grew, the more the enemy attacked. As soon as Naomi and I came together in prayer for God to order our footsteps regarding us moving, the attacks came.

One day while working, I went to call a patient from the lobby. He was about 5'10"-5'11" in height and had a caramel complexion. I was twenty-eight years old and I could tell he was a little older than me, maybe in his early thirties. There was something so different about him and it caused my hands to sweat and butterflies began to form in my stomach. I had been out of my relationship with James for a little over a year. I was still dealing with the hurt from that relationship but there was just something about this man that made me feel like a little girl as I took his blood pressure. I asked him what he was being seen for, reviewed his chart with him and left the room to inform my provider that he was ready to be seen. I had never felt the way I did in that moment towards any other man, not even James. He was on my mind constantly, and I hoped that he would come into the clinic again, but he never did. I shared with my cousin Naomi how I roomed this man I was head over hills for, and how beautiful he was to me. She probably thought

I was crazy at the time to be feeling the way that I did from one encounter with a man I knew nothing about.

Naomi informed me of a basketball and free healthcare event the church would be hosting at a local YMCA for the community. I agreed to volunteer with her taking blood pressures and checking blood sugars. I remember pulling into the YMCA parking lot. As I headed towards the entrance there was a man walking in after me who held the door open for me. When I looked at him to say thank you, it was the same man from the clinic. Well, you can imagine how I felt after I had been daydreaming about him all week! I was so excited and couldn't wait to tell Naomi that he was there. I later learned that he was involved with the basketball tournament. When I pointed him out to Naomi, she informed me that he was actually a friend of hers and that he attended the same church.

After the event, I started to notice him a lot more at church. I even attended a few gatherings and would see him there. Every time I saw him, butterflies constantly developed in my stomach. It was so awkward for me growing silent feelings towards a man that I did not know, nor did he know anything about me. Naomi informed me that there were many women who liked him at church but I wasn't surprised. He was single and a very handsome man. Why wouldn't there be other women interested in him? Because of that, I asked her if she liked him as well but she informed me that she didn't look at him in such a way and only viewed him as a friend. She then informed me about a guy at church who expressed his interest in me and I must say, it took me by surprise. Although she told me about this guy, I still had interest in the guy from the clinic.

I finally got enough courage to reach out to him through social media. I introduced myself and mentioned I was Naomi's cousin. I mentioned that I remembered him from the clinic and that I was the Medical Assistant getting him ready for his visit. I shared that I did not believe my run-ins with him were a coincidence. I believed that God put certain people in my path for a reason and that I wanted us to establish a friendship. It felt so good to finally release what I had been holding in for a while. Unfortunately, he did not respond to my message. I felt so silly and immediately regretted sending him the message. After a few days of checking and hoping he would respond to my message, he never did. I began to ask God to remove all thoughts and emotions I had built towards him. I told myself if he were the man for me, God would show me in His timing. I would not put myself out there again but rather wait for him to approach me.

A couple weeks later, I pulled into the gas station near my home in Saint Paul. I was pulling up to pump eleven when I noticed a guy at pump ten. As I put my truck in park, I looked over at pump ten again and it was him! There were those butterflies again and I was so nervous to get out of my truck. Once again, there we were having another odd run-in. Naomi told me that he lived in Minneapolis, so I just could not believe this man was pumping gas right next to me in

Saint Paul. I waited until he got into his car before I got out of my truck. I was upset for two reasons; one, he never responded to my message and two, I asked God if this man was not for me to remove any feelings I had for him, but they were obviously still there. I just kept running into him and I didn't know if it was a sign or what to make of it. But I was fed up and just asked God to remove how I felt towards him because it was obvious that he had no interest in me. A couple weeks passed and those butterflies were still present when we would walk by one another in church. I found myself writing a poem about him (ridiculous I know!). I finally that realized I needed something to take my mind off him.

I decided to exchange numbers with the man Naomi told me about who had expressed interest in me. He and I started texting and talking over the phone as a way to get to know each other. Although he was a few years younger than I was, he was such a nice person, very handsome and had a lot going for himself. He and I attended a basketball game together and he even invited me over to his home for game nights with some other members from church, including the guy from the clinic. It was a bit awkward being in the same social circle, while still feeling the way I did about him. But at the same time, I was trying to get over it by seeing if something would come out of whatever was happening between me and this other gentleman. However, our communication just didn't go past the friendship line. I knew I desired more than a friendship, but in my heart, I did not believe he was the one for me. Eventually the texting and calling began to decrease, and then stopped all together.

Naomi shared with me that she had been talking to a guy for a couple months and she was starting to have feelings for him. As she shared with me about her developing relationship, I was finally able to get my mind off a love that I never had. One evening Naomi, her sister Andrea, and I decided to have a girl's night out. We were heading out to a jazz event, when Naomi told us that she had to take a rain check. We had just pulled into the parking lot where the event was being held when she called my phone to say she would not be going in. I got out of Andrea's car and walked over to Naomi's car. She told me the man she had been talking to invited her to hang out with him. I was excited for her but sad at the same time. Not only because she was canceling on us, but also because I would have to live vicariously through her new love story. I told her to have fun and that I truly hoped things worked out with him. Andrea and I went on with our night and enjoyed ourselves at the jazz event.

The next day Naomi called me to tell me all about her date. However, I noticed a bit of hesitation in her voice. She started the conversation by saying she did not go on the date with the guy she had been telling me about. But before she could tell me who the guy was that she really went on the date with, I knew. The same man I had told her about since day one of him walking into the clinic, turned out to be the same person she went on a date with the night before. She sounded a bit shocked when I said his name before she could tell me herself. I reminded her that I had asked her in the past if she liked him more than a friend and that she told me no. But for some reason I knew she was not being truthful at the time. All I could do was tell her that I was happy for her as she went into detail about how her night went with him. Although I was furious on the inside, I swallowed my pride as she told me she did like him in the past but he was dating someone at the time. She went on to say that, she had buried her feelings towards him once he started dating and just looked at him as a friend.

She told me how they had been texting each other recently and told me he invited her over to his home. She continued by telling me about meeting his mother that evening and how she spent the night at his home. She told me nothing happened between them, that she laid on his couch as he stared at her while she fell asleep. I was burning with hurt on the inside, but I just could not let her hear it in my voice. Part of me felt that I had no right to be upset about it because he and I never had anything, not to mention he didn't even know me. But at the same time, she was my cousin and I shared with her how I felt about this guy from the beginning. She knew everything but failed to mention anything to me about how she felt about him. I felt she led me to believe she was going on the date with the other guy instead of telling me the truth. Nevertheless, all I could do was end the call by saying I was happy for her.

I will be honest; I was angry and started to develop

bitterness towards her. Subsequently, I started writing her text messages stating how I felt she was sneaky and did not respect me enough to tell me the truth. If she had told me she liked him when I first mentioned him to her, then I wouldn't have looked in his direction twice. I was so angry that I was contemplating about not moving to North Carolina with her anymore. I felt if she would withhold something like that from me, then how could I trust moving out of state with her.

Andrea and I had also grown close over the years, so I talked to her and told her how I felt about the situation. She understood but also didn't want Naomi and me to have a falling out over it. She told me that Naomi would be coming over to her home to wash clothes and that it would be a good idea for me to come over as well. It would give us a chance to hear each other's side of the story. When I arrived, Naomi had not arrived, so I filled Andrea in on the night that she and I went to the Jazz event while Naomi went on the date. When Naomi arrived, we did not speak to one another right away. Andrea had to say something to break the ice and at first the tension was still there. However, after speaking to each other and sharing our feelings, we came to a common ground. She admitted that she should have been honest with me and apologized, I apologized as well for the bitter text messages that I sent.

At the beginning of June, we flew out to North Carolina and this time, Andrea came along with us. We met with the woman from Interim, and after the testing was complete, we were offered the positions. When we returned to Minnesota, things moved quickly for us. We applied for a townhome and were approved for it. It would be available for move in the weekend we were expected to arrive.

As we were preparing ourselves to move, Interim Healthcare contacted us again. They informed us that Duke Hospitals and clinics were on a hiring freeze, which meant they were not hiring anyone from staffing agencies. We were told the freeze could take anywhere from a week to months before they would begin hiring again. We had been so excited that things were coming together but were quickly brought back to square one. We were back to searching for jobs as we continued to work at our current clinic jobs.

My mother kept my daughters during the first visit to North Carolina. After sharing with her that I was considering moving out of state, she initially was excited for me. But as I continued with my plan to move, she started to become very distant towards me. I recall us going on a cruise to the Bahamas that mid-June. A trip that should have been full of great memories was full of nightmares. My uncle paid for the cruise as a way for us to grow closer as a family, but instead ended with my mother cursing me out and accusing me of not caring about her and my siblings. It was so bad that she did not want to be in the same vehicle with me as we traveled back to Minnesota. I was keeping some of my belongings at her home until I moved but that same week she had one of my sisters call me to say she wanted me to come get our things out of her house. As I pulled up, I could see my sisters and brother putting our belongings on the lawn. Apparently, she did not want me to come into her house, so she had them start bringing everything out before I got there. My siblings felt so bad, but I wasn't mad at them or my mother. In the midst of her anger and bad treatment, I was even more determined to move and I had an unusual sense of peace. There were so many reasons for me not to move away from Minnesota. My family didn't want me to move and neither did my children's father. However, I knew I had to do what was best for my daughters and me. I was determined to push through no matter what tried to stop me.

Naomi and I continued to pray and fast together and I believe this is what caused the hand of God to move on our behalf. The enemy knew that God was doing something greater with us. I believe the situation with the man was a distraction and a tactic used to try to get us off course. But what the enemy meant for evil, God turned it around for our good. Interim Healthcare contacted us that same week and let us know that the hiring freeze was over and we could start training that following month in August. We were finally able to close a chapter in our lives, to begin something new and it started with the move to North Carolina.

# Chapter 8
# Stepping out on Faith

*I* called my uncle's phone once more, hoping he was asleep and just didn't hear the phone. Naomi and I had been trying to contact him since the night before with no success. I was feeling a lot of emotion and was unsure of what we were to do next. It was Saturday August 3, 2013. We were due to arrive in North Carolina by that Sunday to move into our townhome and in time for Naomi to begin her training at Duke Hospital. We had been in contact with our uncle who was more than willing to help us move. We were depending on him to help us drive a moving truck and help with paying our deposit for the townhome we were approved for. The initial plan was to leave Friday, but we had been calling his phone back to back with no answer. We finally came to realize, if he were able to help us he would have picked up the phone by now. I looked at Naomi in disbelief, disappointment and anger. Everything had been coming together so well with us moving, then suddenly, we were at a complete stand still.

It was already noon when Naomi looked at me and said we had to make a decision. We were either going to delay our date of moving or step out on faith and totally depend on God to move on our behalf. After giving thought to what we were to do, we finally decided to get on the road. We were leaving my truck parked at her sister's home and our items in storage. Once we were settled in North Carolina, we would come back for the rest of our belongings. We put as much as we could fit into Naomi's Ford Fusion, got our daughters in the car and we were on our way. Just before heading towards North Carolina, we stopped by a grocery store to grab food to eat while on the road. Naomi's sister Andrea met us at the store to say our goodbyes, shared a few tears and we were off.

Naomi drove the first nine hours as we drove through Minnesota, Wisconsin, Illinois, and Indiana. I took over and drove through the rest of Indiana, Ohio, West Virginia and Virginia overnight. While Naomi and the girls were sleeping, I began to get anxious. I had never driven overnight and had fallen asleep behind the wheel in the past. I remember putting William McDowell's worship CD on repeat because I needed to be reminded that Jesus was with me behind the wheel. I was very nervous as I drove through construction and caution signs that read, "Falling rocks" and "Deer". Not to mention I was driving through extremely thick fog at the same time. After driving for a few hours in the fog, I was so relieved to see the sun come up. I could see the beautiful mountains as I drove through the rest of Virginia. I finally started seeing signs for North Carolina and became at ease knowing our destination was ahead of us.

As we pulled into the parking lot of Spring Ridge Apartments nine hours later, a bit of anxiety set in. After filling the gas tank in Naomi's car four times and paying tolls, we had $1000 between the two of us. We had spoken to the property manager prior to us coming and she had informed us that we would need $1895 to move into the townhome. There we were, parked in the parking lot that Sunday morning in North Carolina after driving a little over eighteen hours and we didn't have enough money. Naomi and I walked into the property manager's office informing her that we were the women from Minnesota she had been in contact with. She was happy to know that we made it safely and was ready to get us moved in. We began explaining to her that we only had $1000 and knew we were short $895. I remember having a conversation with her the first time I called. She and I had spoken on the phone for quite a while. I informed her about us moving from out of state and wondered if they had any availability around the date we were looking to move in. She informed me that she had allowed a man to occupy an apartment after his apartment caught fire. She went on to tell me that the he had lost everything and had been sleeping in his car for a couple weeks prior to her allowing him to stay in the apartment. Once he found a place to stay, she had made the apartment available for renting. By her telling me this, I knew she had a good heart and would be willing to help us as well.

She told us the best that she could do was split the deposit amount in half. So instead of needing $1895, we needed to have $1495. We were so grateful to her for being kind enough to lower the deposit amount, but we still needed to come up with $495. We told her we had to make a few phone calls to see if we could come up with the amount. I called my mom, sisters, and even tried calling my uncle but no one answered. Naomi called her mom; she even reached out to a co-worker to no avail. I was willing to pawn my laptop; however, the pawnshops were closed on Sundays.

Naomi called her sister Andrea but she did not answer. She made mention that Andrea was probably in church at the time and could not pick up her phone. In that moment, we went into prayer mode. We knew that God would not forsake us after literally stepping out on faith, knowing that we did not have enough money to move into the townhome. However, we knew that God was going to provide some way.

I remember looking at cars pulling into the parking lot, wondering if God was going to have someone pull up to Naomi's car and bless us with the $495 that we needed. Then, Naomi's phone rang. It was Andrea returning her phone call. Naomi explained to her that we made it to North Carolina and were trying to get moved into the townhome but were short $495. I couldn't hear what Andrea said on the other end of the phone, but I remember Naomi's facial expression changing as she hung up her phone. She started digging in her purse as I asked her what Andrea said. She said Andrea instructed her to dig deep inside her purse and call her back. I looked at her with confusion as to why she would tell her to do such a thing. Then Naomi pulled a white envelope from her purse. When she opened the envelope, there was a letter along with $500.

My mouth dropped in disbelief of what she was holding in her hand. After traveling for hours on the road and going into Naomi's purse multiple times, we had never come across the envelope. In that moment, I believed it was not meant for us to see the envelope while we were on the road because we probably would have spent the money. We both just started to thank God, screaming and crying all at the same time. God knew the need and had supplied it already without us even knowing. When Andrea came to say goodbye to us at the grocery store, before we headed to North Carolina, she slipped the envelope in Naomi's purse without us noticing. She later shared that God instructed her to give money as a going away gift. However, she was having a financial struggle at the time. When God revealed the amount, she realized she had to give it because the money did not belong to her anyway. It belonged to God, so through her obedience, we were able to move into the apartment.

We walked into the leasing office with tears of joy, as we told the apartment manager that we had the money needed to move into the apartment. We shared with her what happened which brought her to tears as well. Then she asked, "Do you all have money to eat?" We were so happy to have the money to move in, that we hadn't considered that but we knew God would provide. She looked at us and handed us back the money order; she told us to use the money for food and anything else we would need until we could get our belongings from Minnesota! Not only were we able to purchase a few groceries along with paper plates, cups and utensils, but she even reached out to a friend of hers that would be able to help us with getting mattresses and a few lamps. We were in total shock as she handed us the keys to the townhome.

We could not stop praising God for how He provided for us far beyond what either one of us could have imagined. Naomi began training the next day. I stayed home with the girls for that first three weeks just until they started school and would start my training closer to the end of August. After going from sleeping on the carpet for a week to sleeping on air mattresses, our uncle finally called us. He admitted he did not know how to tell us he was not able to help us at the time. However, I believe God did not allow him to help us; He wanted us to depend completely on Him so that He would get all the glory. A couple of months later, I flew back to Minnesota for my uncle to help drive a moving truck with the rest of our belongings to North Carolina.

During that short visit, my daughters' father, James had just been released for prison. We had visited him one last time before moving. Although he and I were no longer together, I needed to get his blessing to move our daughters out of state. I just would not have been at peace without consulting him first. He didn't want us to move but agreed and understood I needed to do what I believed was best for us. I assured him that I would take care of them. He and his brothers even helped take our things out of storage and packed them on the truck. God has such a way of doing things; I believe I needed to see James to know that I was no longer in love with him. It was as if I was finally closing that chapter of my life. I said my goodbyes and was off to meet my uncle to get on the road for my final drive from Minnesota to North Carolina.

# Chapter 9

# With Every Elevation Comes Retaliation

*A*lthough I was relieved that we were finally able to get settled, I had known deep down inside that North Carolina was temporary for my daughters and me. Texas was always in the back of my mind. I knew eventually we would make our way there, but for some reason God needed me in North Carolina in this season.

There was a lot I was still dealing with from my last relationship and a lot of growth I needed in order for God to be able to use me and move me to my next destination. I was happy to finally be in North Carolina, but also not satisfied because I had let go of everything in Minnesota. I let go of my engagement, my house, and moved away from family. At the time, I felt like I was losing everyone and everything I knew by moving twenty hours away but not gaining anything. I had no idea the obstacles that laid ahead of me. The many tears I would cry or the season of lack and loneliness, that would creep into my life. I didn't see how this was going to help me by moving my daughters away from all they had ever known to follow Christ. I depended on my family's love and I depended on my daughters' father being in their lives. Nevertheless, God was slowly showing me that He wanted me to depend on Him and Him alone. I was learning God bruises, but He binds up; He wounds, but His hands make whole and it was my season of preparation.

As we entered the church, we were greeted by smiling faces and it was so welcoming. Someone from Minnesota had recommended that we visit the church and had heard wonderful things about the pastor. It was our first Sunday attending since moving to North Carolina. It was an awesome service; the pastor and first lady were very friendly. We had been in search of a church home, so after a couple weeks of attending I was ready to join but Naomi felt differently.

One Sunday, we could sense that the presence of the Lord was high and Naomi was just basking in the presence of God. Even as service ended, she was still kind of out of it. I remember one of the altar workers coming to me saying that I should pull the car up to the door because she may need some help getting into the car. I left out of the building, but as I pulled up to the door, Naomi was walking out. I thought it was weird because I had just walked out as she was still worshiping. As she got in the car and I could tell something was wrong. She said someone in the sanctuary told her she had to leave. I looked at her in shock! The church we attended back in Minnesota was a church where we could praise and worship God as long as we needed even after service had ended. You never know what God is doing, so you never want to interrupt someone's praise or worship.

Naomi expressed that she no longer wanted to attend the church. I insisted that she speak with the pastor regarding what happened. She was not interested because she did not want to join the church from the beginning.

I told her that I would speak to the pastor regarding what happened just so no one else would have to experience what she had. After speaking with the pastor, he apologized and stated that was not how the church operated. He understood Naomi not wanting to come back but wanted to speak with her. In the meantime, I continued to attend the church as Naomi visited other churches to no avail. She had finally had her meeting with the pastor; I was relieved because I wanted her to start attending the church with me again. I didn't want that experience to stop her from coming and maybe after speaking to the pastor she would change her mind. Well, I was wrong. After the meeting, she expressed to me how the pastor told her that he was not sure if what she was saying was true. He told her that she did not have to attend the church any more. Our conversations were literally like night and day. He seemed so sincere when I spoke with him, but when she spoke to him it was the complete opposite. From that point on, I decided not to attend either. I just did not believe God wanted us to worship in separate churches. So, we began to stream our church in Minnesota online from home.

A couple weeks later, I woke up to hearing water running. I figured Naomi was up getting ready for work. When I came out of my room, I could still hear the water running but the sound was not coming from her room. I was hearing it running from downstairs. As I made my way down the steps, I could see water gushing out of the back of the downstairs' bathroom toilet. I could see water covering the entire downstairs floor. We were still getting settled in the townhome, so we still had boxes on the floor that were now soaked in water. When I called maintenance, they were next door in our neighbor's home because the water coming from our townhome had seeped into her home. Luckily, they found a way to stop the water from running. They had to vacuum the majority of the water and placed fans in our home to get it completely dried.

Due to some of our belongings being damaged from the water, we met with the apartment manager to discuss the renter's insurance we had signed up for with their office. However, the type of renter's insurance we had only covered the property of the townhome and would not cover any of our things that had water damage. But when we signed the lease, we were under the impression that the insurance would cover our belongings as well. Unfortunately, there was nothing more that could be done regarding the lack of coverage for our damaged items. She stated the best thing she could do was move us into an upgraded townhome. The upgraded townhome was much nicer than the one we were currently in so we agreed to move. We moved all of our things from the flooded townhome into the new townhome. Just when I had gotten over the whole flood issue, I didn't think anything else could go wrong.

My daughter TeMari came home from school one day and told me that a boy in her classroom said that he would bring his father's gun to school to shoot her and two other children that were in her class. I became worried about my daughter's safety so I went to her school the next day and spoke with the principal. She informed me that she had already spoken to the student's parents and that he was being suspended from the school for a few days.

We hadn't fully settled into the townhome when TeMari came to me complaining that her armpits were hurting. I thought the area of where she was complaining about was odd and assumed she may have hurt herself while playing. But when she went to sleep that night, she woke up screaming. She just kept saying her armpits were hurting. I examined her body from head to toe and nothing unusual stood out. However, when I asked her to open her mouth, I saw white spots on the back of her throat and knew immediately that she had strep throat. I took her to an urgent care where she tested positive for strep and was started on an antibiotic. I was informed that the pain in her armpits was more likely due to her having swollen lymph nodes, which can be caused by the strep. But the very next day she developed a rash all over her body and I noticed her skin was peeling. I kept calm on the outside; but I was panicking on the inside. I just didn't understand what was going on with my daughter. I assumed she was having an allergic reaction to the antibiotic so I took her into the clinic again and was given a different antibiotic for her. As the day progressed, her skin continued to peel and she was crying asking me what was wrong with her. I began praying for God to give me understanding of what was happening to her. I took her in again, but this time to a children's hospital and I was determined not to leave until I clarity about my daughter's health.

There was a resident who came into the room to see us. I informed him of her strep diagnosis and explained what symptoms she was still having. He examined her and then he stepped out of the room. He came back with the provider that he was shadowing. He asked me some questions as he examined her, then they stepped out of the room once again. About twenty minutes later, they came back into the room and diagnosed her with a virus called Scarlet Fever. He set down with me and showed me the stages of the virus, which she had already gone through. The skin peeling was the final stage and meant the Scarlet Fever had already taken its course. He informed me that it had developed because of her sensitivity to the bacteria of the strep throat. He said her skin would continue to peel for weeks but the worse of it was over. I was so relieved to finally know and understand what was going on with her.

Although TeMari's skin continued to peel, she was back to being her happy self and was able to go back to school. I was so grateful that she was better and I wouldn't have to miss any more days of work. I knew with the days I had already missed due to staying home with her would leave me with a short paycheck. It was nice to have flexibility with the temp agency, but not working meant not getting paid. Not to mention my assignment at my current clinic was ending. When the agency informed me of a new clinic assignment I would be working, I was excited because I would able to have a full paycheck. It was another fulltime clinic assignment and I was going to be there for at least one month.

Since moving to North Carolina, Naomi had been working at the same clinic but I was already on my third clinic assignment. When I started the new clinic assignment, I started off working a full week. Then the following week, the clinic manager informed me that they would no longer need me to work a full week due to the clinic being slow unexpectedly. They had me working three days a week at the most. I was disappointed because I was already having trouble making ends meet after missing work due to TeMari's illness. I was really starting to feel that moving us to North Carolina was the wrong decision. First, the flood in the townhome, then my daughter getting scarlet fever, now I was struggling financially and we still hadn't found a church to attend.

One day after being sent home due to a slow day at the clinic, there was an announcement on the radio regarding a church having a book signing. The title of the book was something about soul ties, which caught my attention. Naomi and I had recently discussed soul ties and I wanted to learn more, so I decided I would go to the book signing that weekend and surprise Naomi with a copy of the book as well. I had just made it home when a woman that lived next door to us saw me getting out of my truck. She informed me that she was a friend of our former neighbor, whose home was also affected by the flood. I told her that we had moved from another state and were trying to get settled before the flood hit us. . I went on to tell her about the challenging time we were having finding a church home. She then began to tell me about her church and invited us to attend that following Sunday.

Ironically, it turned out to be the same church I had just heard about on the radio that was having the book signing. I told her that I was going to purchase our copies of the book and that would give me a chance to get a feel of the church and that we may also visit that following Sunday. Pulling up to the church, I noticed there weren't many vehicles in the parking lot. I walked into the doors of the church but they were still setting up for the book signing. I was the first person to arrive and was greeted by one of the deacons. He seated me in the sanctuary until the pastor and first lady were ready. As I sat in the sanctuary, it reminded me of our home church and I had a sense of peace. After meeting the pastor and first lady, they seemed very nice as they signed our books. I had such a great feeling about the church. When I returned home, I surprised Naomi with her book. I told her how our neighbor invited us to visit the church and she agreed.

Walking in the sanctuary of the church, the purple and gold colors made the church resemble our church in

Minnesota. After streaming service online for weeks, it felt good to finally be back in the house of the Lord. After hearing an awesome word from the pastor, he began to close out service with an altar call. After altar call, Pastor asked if there was anyone that needed a church home and to raise their hand if they were interested in joining the church. Initially, we did not raise our hands, but it was what he said next that prompted us to join. He said if there was anyone that had been streaming church online; they could no longer continue to stream and needed to join! I felt so convicted and told Naomi that we needed to join. We walked down to the altar, joined and have been there since.

We had finally gotten settled into the upgraded townhome when Naomi informed me that her sister Andrea had decided to move to North Carolina. We began to plan a trip back to Minnesota within the next couple months to help move her down, when we received news that our uncle's daughter was diagnosed with cancer. In March of 2014, Naomi and I traveled back to Minnesota to help Andrea move to North Carolina. During the time of us being there, we told that our cousin was in the hospital. We were only going to be in Minnesota for a brief time, but knew we had to make our way to see her. Although it was hard seeing my cousin in the state she was in, she was a fighter and was in good spirits most of the time we were there.

She told us that she had been having stomach pain for five months off and on, but one day while at work she collapsed with excruciating pain. She was transported from work by the ambulance to the hospital where they ran several tests. She had imaging done and a tumor was found behind her pancreas. She said she had radiation treatment called radio embolization to try shrinking the tumor with no improvement. Chemotherapy was not done because although she said it may shrink the tumors; the it would cause her to lose hair and she would become sicker, which could potentially kill her. By that time, the cancer had already spread causing her to have bone, lung and liver cancer. She was told that there was nothing else that could be done and advised to go home and get a hospice nurse.

Five years ago, her older sister, who was in her early thirties at the time, was a cancer survivor. She shared her story with the family during a funeral for another cousin that was diagnosed with colon cancer in her twenties, but had passed away. It was as if our younger generation was being attacked in their twenties with a type of cancer that usually is not screened until around the age of forty.

She explained to us that we should have genetic testing due to our family carrying a gene called Familial Adenomatous Polyposis (FAP). It was the main condition that caused cancer within our family. It was such a blessing to be able to have that time with her and to receive this information to be able to tell the rest of our family. We prayed with her, said our goodbyes and were on the road the next day heading back to North Carolina.

The week after we returned, I received a new assignment at the Colorectal Cancer Center in Raleigh. My very first day of walking into the office, I saw books full of information regarding FAP. The same information my cousin had shared with us was in these booklets. I knew it was no coincidence that I was there and that I needed to soak up as much information as I could while being there. I spoke with the Genetic Counselor that was working at the office and was given so much information to share with our family.

In that moment, I understood that moving to North Carolina was not in vain and realized that what God was doing was not about us. He was showing me it was much bigger than us. Most of our family members were not seeking the ways of God. Naomi, Andrea, and I were the only ones in our immediate families following Christ. Not only had He called us; we were His chosen. He was bringing us together to do His work. He was going to do great works through us because we desired His will for not only our lives, but for our family.

In October 2014, seven months after our visit, our cousin passed away at twenty-eight years old. This was the second death of a family member dying from cancer in their twenties. However, I believed God was going to use us to break generational curses off our family.

# Chapter 10

# Who I Am

*D*uring church service one Sunday, Naomi told me the Lord placed my name on her heart as the guest speaker preached on affliction. To say that I was "going through" was an understatement. When I asked God to teach me His ways and let His will be done in my life, He started to purge, prune and show me my wicked heart.

Prior to moving to North Carolina, I had made a vow before God that I would not give my body to anyone else until marriage. This was coming from someone who was overcoming a sixteen year addiction to masturbation and pornography for sixteen years. Before my daughters' father was sentenced to prison, he was the only man I was intimate with for six years. But a few months after letting go of our relationship, I had sex with someone else and regretted it. I continued to watch pornography and masturbate. However, months after being baptized, I started to feel guilty after masturbating. I would cry and feel so dirty after doing it. My eyes were now open spiritually and I knew that what I was doing was not pleasing to God. After feeling a great deal of conviction and the weight of sixteen years of shame on me, by the grace of God, I stopped masturbating, I disciplined myself to no longer watch pornography and stopped listening to certain types of music to prevent the desire to please myself. From that day forward, I asked God to have His way in my life, to replace my desires with His desires. It was then that God began to show me who I am in Him.

God was stripping me of many things and I was going through a very painful process of transformation. Even though what I was going through was for my good, I was very taken aback by it. God's plan was not the way I expected it to be. I was still struggling financially and at times going back and forth about whether I made the right decision to move away from Minnesota. I was constantly going to God in prayer about everything I wanted my life to be. I started feeling bad for myself. I felt like I was a bad mother for moving my daughters away from their father. I remember asking God to work on James's heart and bring us back together but then the next minute I would ask Him to remove any feelings I still had for him. I thought I had failed my mother because she was still upset and not talking to me for moving away with her granddaughters. I was dealing with rejection and my emotions were all over the place. I didn't realize that I was playing tug of war with God. I was asking Him to have His way in my life, but I was still trying to control it. I thought I was being tortured and felt I had done something wrong. I couldn't have been further from the truth. God began to show me that He did not bring me out of darkness into His marvelous light to feel defeated.

These things were causing me to lean on God and drawing me closer to Him. He was teaching me how to pray not only for myself but also for my family. I was at the altar almost every Sunday and in my closet most mornings before work as He taught me how to worship him. I started fasting once a week as a way of dying to my flesh and growing deeper in the Holy Spirit. I was changing mentally, physically and spiritually. Over the past year, I had lost close to fifty pounds. I decided to change my eating habits because I wanted to live a healthier lifestyle and due to the family history of cancer. I had already been natural with no chemicals in my hair for over a year when I decided to grow locs. I was transforming right before my very own eyes.

I became active in ministry at church. I was serving as an usher; I was in the choir and a praise dancer. But God was constantly putting me through tests, one of the biggest was with my daughters' father James. I had finally gotten over my six-year relationship with James and it took me two years to do it. But how could I explain to my ex fiancé that God had changed me and that I was now living a sold out life for Christ? Before he went to prison, I lived the same lifestyle he did but during the time of his absence, God began dealing with me. God started showing me that He had a greater plan for my life. He had taken me away from everything I had ever known to grow and shape me into the woman He had called me to be.

I ended our engagement while he was in prison, moved to another state and started a whole new life serving God. There aren't many single mothers that can say they would have done what I did. Heck, I wouldn't have done what I did if I did not believe God instructed me to do it. In the beginning, it had been an emotional roller coaster. I had cried so many tears, asking God why He had me to end my relationship. It was one of the worst times of my life because I was hurt and I did not agree with God. But God had revealed to me that He never ordained that relationship in the first place. I created that relationship. I made the decision to have children with him and during that time, God had nothing to do with our relationship.

So, one day while on a social media website, I came across pictures of him and his new girlfriend. I received phone calls from concerned family members, and even had a talk with Naomi about it. She told me that she would be angry about the situation, if she were me. The woman he was currently with was someone I had associated with in the past. She knew who I was and I was sure she knew he was my daughters' father. But as I looked at their pictures, I wasn't angry or bitter. I just began to bring their relationship in prayer and hoped for the best in both of their lives. A week before I saw the pictures of them together, James sent me a text. In the text was a picture of who I used to be with a drink and a cigar in my hand. At the bottom of the picture, it read, "Do you miss me at all?" But I responded with an encouraging message that let him know that I was no longer that woman in the picture. I told him if it was God's will for us to be together, then He would have to bring us back together. The following week I found out about his relationship.

When James sent me that picture message, God showed me the very reason I needed to close the door to my past, and that I was being delivered. Out of our messy relationship, God created two beautiful twin girls. He was creating a beautiful friendship between James and I, and our daughters even started spending the summers with him in Minnesota. When James's relationship ended, he would tell our daughters that he still loved me and wanted to marry me. Hearing him say these things would make me wonder, from time to time, if there was still any chance of us getting back together. Especially when my daughters told me when they returned home one summer that he was attending church. My daughters told me their father had a new girlfriend, and how they'd spent the majority of their summer at her home with their dad and her three children. Their sharing this with me caught me off guard because I was still under the impression that James was no longer in a relationship. When my daughters told me her name, it turned out to be the same name of the woman James cheated on me with when he and I were engaged. Over the past few years, he and I developed a great friendship, so I thought to myself that she couldn't possibly be the same woman he was with that caused our six-year relationship to end. But deep down inside I knew she was and I felt betrayed. Not only because of who she was, but also now, my daughters were involved. They expressed how much they liked her and had established a relationship with her and her children over the summer. But I also felt the need to confirm with him whether or not she was the same woman.

A couple weeks had gone by since the girls returned home and I hadn't built up the courage to ask James about his new girlfriend. Every time he called, I would hand the phone over to the girls without saying a word to him because I was hurt and didn't want him to know it. I thought I was completely healed from our relationship. After all, it had been five years since our relationship ended, but my heart was hurting. One day, I was so bothered as I was preparing to leave for church service that I ended up in the middle of my bedroom floor, crying my eyes out. I would later learn I was not completely healed and was actually grieving over the death of our relationship.

As I cried on my bedroom floor, the Holy Spirit instructed me to pray for James, his girlfriend and her children. In that moment, I began to pray without stopping. I prayed for James in a way I had not prayed for him before and that if his relationship with this woman was drawing him closer to God, then for God to have His way. I prayed for her and asked God to not allow James to hurt her the way he hurt me and for him to be faithful to her. I prayed for her children, as if they were my own children asking God to cover them and to supply all their needs. When I was finally finished, I could tell the heaviness that was on my heart was lighter, but was still there. I managed to get off the floor and make it to church to receive a powerful word that moved me closer to complete healing. That day, I learned that when God delivers a person from something, that area must be replaced with something else and cannot be left empty. If not, the very thing that was removed may come back and make the condition of that person worse than it was in the beginning. Therefore, I began asking God to deliver me from the grief I was dealing with and to replace it with joy.

Later that week, while attending a small group bible study, the leader of the group had us all gather around in a circle with our hands together for prayer and to give our prayer requests. I briefly shared how I had recently learned that grief not only comes from the death of a person, but can develop from the death of a relationship and that I was seeking God to deliver me from grief. As the leader prayed and mentioned the prayer requests each individual stated, I began praying inwardly. I did not utter a word aloud, but in my heart I asked God to remove every drop of grief and replace it with a continuous flow of joy. As I said these words repeatedly in my spirit, the small group leader came over to me and laid her hands on me. She began speaking the exact words I was saying in my heart. She kept declaring that my heart be filled with a continuous flow of joy and all I could do was cry. I knew God was revealing my heart to her and that night, by faith I knew I was being healed from grief.

I knew I was healed when James called and I finally asked him if the woman he was seeing was, in fact, the same woman he cheated on me with years ago. Although I already knew the answer, I still needed to hear him say it. As he said yes, I was not shocked nor moved by his words. He, on the other hand, began asking me how I felt about him being with her and how some of the people we both knew in Minnesota felt I should hate him. If we had spoken any sooner, who knows how I would have reacted. However, because God completely healed my heart, I was able to honestly say that I did not hate him and that I was praying for God's best for him. I told him how I appreciated her love for my daughters and how they adored her. I told him not to expect us to become best friends, but to know that I was happy for him.

I made up in my mind that I would not settle and would continue being faithful in my singleness. Although I desired marriage, I knew in God's timing, he had something far greater in store for me. He had not only given me understanding but also leaders who were notable examples of what a marriage should be.

At times, I dealt with wanting to be married and having a male figure around for my daughters. I began to pray a list of all the things I wanted my future husband to be. Then I realized that if I trusted God to write my love story this time around, I needed to focus on myself. So instead of praying for all the things I wanted my future husband to be, I began praying for God to make me a wife. The Bible says, "He who finds a wife finds a good thing." Therefore, I needed to develop into a good wife. During this process, I began to feel hidden. I felt as if I was like a caterpillar in a cocoon. God was developing me in my singleness into a woman of God, wife, mother, writer and so much more. I was growing in Him and He had given me many men and women to help me along the way. I was being made whole, learning to love myself and accepting the things I could not change about myself. I became conscious of the way I spoke and carried myself. I knew I was my daughters' first teacher and that they were watching my every move. I learned that I needed to be wise with the words I spoke regarding our lives. The Bible says, "Life and death are in the power of the tongue," so I began speaking God's promises over our lives and over the lives of my family.

I began seeing myself as a writer and started meeting other writers at church. My stylist who locked my hair was a writer, as well, with a published book and I even met a few patients who were writers as well. Since I was currently working in the medical field, I started to consider enrolling in school for journalism to sharpen my writing skills. I figured that getting a journalism degree would open doors to the field of writing and would transition me out of the medical field. I applied to North Carolina Agricultural and Technical State University, as it was one of two accredited universities in North Carolina for journalism. I knew I wanted to get started because it would take me about four years to obtain the degree. I was excited and ready to start this journey with school.

I was finally starting to see who I was in Christ and believe that the move to North Carolina was necessary for my growth and to become the successful woman I have always desired to be. For the first time in my life, I saw I had a purpose for being and this was the fuel I needed to keep pushing towards the mark of my calling. This was not only for me, but also for my daughters, my siblings and everyone else that was connected to my life. All of what I had been through and was going through was good for me. My mess was being shaped into my message, which is my testimony of going from who I was to who I am. My first step was to get accepted to North Carolina Agricultural and Technical State University, to graduate with a Bachelor's Degree in Journalism and be sharpened into the great writer I was chosen to be.

# Chapter 11

## The Seed Planter

*G*od had revealed to me that He would be doing a shift in me by having me write many books. However, I was still working as a temp in the medical field floating to different clinics. I knew there was a purpose behind why He had me where I was. But I was growing tired of being in that field of work when I knew He was doing something new within me. As I continued to be floated to different clinics, each morning I began asking God to order my footsteps and show me what my purpose was in my assigned clinic.

There was a day I was assigned to work in the vascular department of the clinic I had been assigned to for the past few months. I had never worked in this department before so I had no idea what to expect. As patients came in to be seen, I was assigned to review each patient's medication list to make sure their medications were current. As I logged into a computer to get ready for the next patient, my coworker was bringing a woman into the room that recently had surgery performed on her leg for gangrene in her foot. However, the staples from her surgery site had come open while she was using the bathroom. She had left a trail of blood from the bathroom into the exam room. I silently looked on in shock as blood continued to flow out of her surgery site. My coworker left the room to clean up the blood. As she left, I began to feel a tug on my heart to pray with the patient, and it was an overwhelming feeling that I could not shake.

Now this was something I had never done in the work place so I did not move right away. I continued logging into the computer as I contemplated on whether the patient would be offended or if I would be putting my job at risk. As I stood up to grab gauze out of the cabinet to help absorb the blood leaking from her incision, I turned around to the patient and asked, "Can I pray with you"? The patient looked up at me with tears in her eyes and said "please?" I knew this was God's doing but I was so nervous and didn't know how to begin praying for her. I opened prayer by asking the Holy Spirit to give me the words to say and allowed the Him to pray through me. Once we said Amen, the patient thanked me. I gave her a hug and spoke a few words of encouragement as the provider walked into the exam room.

I helped the provider with getting her bleeding under control until my coworker came in to take over. During my lunch break, I sat and thought about what had just taken place and could not believe what I had done. But I believed what I felt the Holy Spirit lead me to do and although I hesitated at first, I was obedient. Only God knows why He led me to pray for that woman that day but from then on, God began to show me my purpose for being in the medical field.

Over the next few weeks, my pastor began preaching on a topic entitled, "Are You Anointed for This?" with different subtopics. But, this particular Sunday, he preached on the subtopic entitled, "Are You Anointed for Their Conditions?" He preached about many people that are dealing with different infirmities, sicknesses, and diseases. He was teaching us that we must be anointed to deal with the many conditions that people are facing. God was speaking to me through that message as my purpose in the medical field began to fully unfold. I found myself praying with patients as the Holy Spirit led me, I was no longer nervous because I was on a mission to plant seeds of faith in the hearts of those that were ready to give up. I met many patients that were dealing with certain conditions that caused them to struggle to function daily.

I began writing the names of patients that I needed to continue to pray for outside of the workplace. Within six months, I had floated to several different clinics. I prayed with many patients during this time, planting seeds of faith, and giving words of encouragement. One clinic that really touched me was an eating disorder clinic. I was there on an assignment for two weeks. There were children from the age of eleven to eighteen years old dealing with insecurities about their bodies and not wanting to eat due to being concerned with gaining weight. It hurt me so much to see these children dealing with this at such a young age. I would get on my face and cry before God praying for them. There were some children that stood out more than others and I would continuously mention their names in prayer.

As I prayed and spoke encouraging words to those in need, by faith, I knew God was going to bring the increase. He would bring increase in knowledge of His presence in their lives. I believed He would increase their faith, strength, and hope in Him. God was using me to be a light in those dark places and to make others aware that we are not to just put our trust in human beings, but in God. I encouraged them to increase their faith in knowing that God is our ultimate healer. I hoped that they would one day open their mouths to pray and to seek God regarding their conditions and that He would bring forth His healing power and show His might in their lives.

God continued to use me to plant seeds in many other clinics. I would leave knowing that I may not see the manifestation of my prayers with the patients I encountered. But it was well with my soul to know that God saw me fit to be used as a seed planter. I had comfort in knowing that only God could bring forth the increase as I shared His love and goodness with those who were in need.

One day after church service, Naomi, the girls and I were coming out of a grocery store when we saw a homeless young man. He looked like he was in his early twenties and he resembled my little brother. As we walked passed, I read his sign that said, "Anything would help" and I felt a tug on my heart to reach out to him. We continued walking towards Naomi's car and began pulling out of the parking space to head home. However, as we were leaving the parking lot, I told Naomi we needed to go back and talk to him. Naomi looked at me with uncertainty while asking if I was sure. I assured her I was and that it was a feeling I could not shake. I just knew in my heart that we needed to help this young man in any way that we could.

As we walked up to him, I introduced myself and he told us his name was Sonny. We sat down on the ground in our Sunday's best, talking to him as he told us how he ended up homeless. He shared with us that he had a younger sister that was homeless as well and he was trying to get enough money to get them a hotel room. We gave him money to go towards the hotel room and even bought him a pizza after he mentioned being hungry. We prayed with him, gave him a hug and went on our way.

When we got home, Naomi remembered a man we met at a back to school event for the girls and felt she was being led to contact him regarding Sonny. She called him and went into detail regarding the young man, explaining that he and his sister had nowhere to stay. Ironically, the man owned a five-bedroom home that he would allow individuals with no place to stay to live until they were back on their feet. He just so happened to have one vacant room. He was willing to allow the young man to stay as long as he was willing to work on getting his life back on track.

Naomi and I were so ecstatic that we rushed to her car and drove back to the grocery store to tell Sunny about the man we spoke with that had a room available for him and his sister at no charge. As we pulled up, we saw him still sitting outside of the store. We got out of the car and explained to him the good news. He was so shocked and agreed to check out the home. We helped him pick up his belongings and drove him to the man's house. When we pulled up to the home, the man that Naomi spoke to over the phone greeted us. The house was very nice and as we walked in, we could smell food being prepared. The room that Sonny would be staying in had one full size bed with a closet and dresser. Sonny agreed to stay and expressed his gratitude towards us, but I knew it was the Lord working through us. He informed us that his sister was at a local shelter and asked if we could drop him off there. As we took him to the shelter, he informed us that he had enough money for him and his sister to take the bus to get back to the home. He thanked us; we exchanged numbers and told him to contact us if he needed anything. That was the last time we spoke with him. But from then on, my life was changed as I was finally living a purpose filled life being about my Father's business.

I had begun working at a bookstand for the pastor and first lady of the church I attended. I was selling the many relationship books they had written. Pastor was having free luncheons where he taught about social, family, and intimate relationships. As I signed people up for the luncheons, some people began to open up to me about their situations. Some were struggling with family relationships, some had been divorced, and some had marriages that were near divorce.

Although I had never been married, being in a relationship for six years and engaged for three of those years gave me enough insight. It was like a marriage without the title and felt like I had gone through a divorce without the court battle. But God used me to minister to them right in the middle of the mall and I would go home bringing their names and their situations before God in prayer. While serving my Pastor's vision, I was learning a lot about my own vision. I was ready to walk in the promise of being a bestselling author.

# Chapter 12

# God's Most Valuable Princesses

*I* received an email from one of my daughter's computer lab teachers, expressing her concern about some pictures my daughter created during computer class at school. She shared that after my daughter was finished with the computer, another child went to log on but couldn't because my daughter was still logged in. As the teacher logged her out, she noticed the names of pictures my daughter saved on the computer and was very concerned. Because I was at work, I agreed to have her send the pictures to my email so I could see exactly what she was concerned about.

When I received the pictures, there were five pictures my daughter saved under five different names. The names they were saved under were "bed," "comeing," "kiss," "sexy," and "neked." By reading these names, I could clearly see why her computer teacher contacted me. I sat there in shock because although my daughter misspelled a couple of the words; it was obvious of what she was trying to spell. The entire time I was at work, my mind continued wondering why in the world she would choose those words out of all the words she knew. When I arrived home after work, I approached my daughter about the pictures but she could not give me a reason why she had chosen those names.

I asked her if she had heard me use them, heard them on a movie, heard them used by any of the teens who were their baby-sitters, or she heard them from one of our cousins, but she insisted she hadn't. However, I knew deep down inside, there was a root to where this was coming from.

When confronting my daughters about something, the majority of the time they have no problem being honest with me. But every now and then, I would catch them in a lie. When this happens, I would always remind them of that saying, "What's done in the dark will always be brought to the light" and that and God would eventually reveal to me whatever it was they were not being truthful about. A couple months had gone by after the computer lab incident and although no other incidents occurred, it was something that still lingered in the back of my mind.

One day Naomi, Andrea and I were sitting at the living room table in our apartment just having a conversation while my daughters and little cousin were upstairs in their room, listening to music from a tablet. The only music I would allow my daughters to listen to was primarily gospel and some songs from artists they would hear on the Disney Channel. But as we sat at the kitchen table, I could hear the girls listening to a song that I had heard before while at work when the providers would listen to different music stations. I knew the lyrics to the song were inappropriate, so I called them downstairs. As they approached me, I told them the song they were listening to was not a "kid friendly" song. So I grabbed the tablet to turn off the song when they began to reach for it insisting they could turn it off. I thought it was strange the way they reacted so I proceeded to turn it off anyway.

As I removed the song, I could see the history of other things that were being looked up on the tablet. Suddenly, my stomach dropped as if I was on a rollercoaster ride as I read what they had been viewing. They had looked up things such as "boy kissing girl" and "boy touching girl's boobs." I immediately passed the tablet to Naomi and Andrea to see what I saw and they had the same reactions. I began yelling at them out of anger and confusion, asking why they had been looking up such things. I could see the fear in their eyes and that they were too afraid to say anything. I literally walked away from the table, rushed into my bedroom and began to cry. My mind could not wrap around what I saw and my emotions were through the roof.

Several minutes later, I was able to pull myself together and suppressed my emotions. Although I was still fuming with hurt and anger, I managed to go out to the living room and speak with them. I needed to know why they had been looking up these things that their eight-year old minds could barely comprehend. During the time I was in my room, Andrea had been speaking with the girls trying to get to the underlining issue and even had them write apology letters to me. While speaking with them, they stated they looked up "boy kissing girl," and from there different videos popped up associated with it and out of curiosity they looked at other images. As they shared this with me, I now understood where my daughter came up with the names she saved those pictures under in her computer class. But it also showed me that this was a seed that was trying to grow in her mind because it was affecting her at school.

In that very moment, the Holy Spirit reminded me of my own struggles that I had been delivered from and how the same issue was trying to grab hold of my daughters. A fire began to rise on the inside of me. It wasn't so much anger, but rather a passion to dismantle whatever the enemy was trying to do with my daughters and how I needed to protect their purity. I knew God brought the issue to the light not for me to feel defeated or that I failed as a parent, but He was making me aware of it so that I could do something about it. Due to pornography being a click of a button away, I was not certain of the type of images they had been exposed to. I desperately needed God's strength and guidance, so I knew I had a lot of praying and fasting to do. However, I also had some practical steps to take in order to uproot that seed from their minds.

We met with First Lady from our church through her counseling center where she, along with her team, counseled families dealing with different life challenges. My daughters would be able to meet with a licensed therapist who specialized in counseling children. During the initial visit, I was able to open up to First Lady about my concerns. I even shared with her my fears because of my own past struggles and how I was ready to do whatever I needed in order to prevent them from going down the same path I did. After speaking with her, I received a sense of comfort. I was confident in knowing that God would not have revealed it if He hadn't already given us the victory over it.

I met with the therapist first, and then the therapist met with my daughters privately. We had a total of three sessions with her and at the end she sat down with me to assure me that everything was going to be fine. She understood my concerns about the images they were exposed to. She stated that after speaking with them, she could see that this was something they had come across unintentionally while looking up something like "boy kissing girl" which should have been harmless. She encouraged me to have discussions with them so they would not view sex as a "bad" thing, but to inform them that it is something God created for adults who are married. Also, for me to talk about the images they saw in a language they could understand and to inform them that the world has tainted what God created by making these inappropriate images. She stated my daughters were not the only children who had experienced seeing inappropriate images online and that she had seen far worse cases. I knew she was not trying to minimize the issue, but more so trying to give me a level of peace about the situation. Overall, the sessions were very helpful. She was able to get me to view the situation from a different perspective when it came to talking with them about it. I no longer felt awkward and was given a strategy of how to speak with them.

A few months went by of not allowing them to have access to their tablets out of fear that they would come across those images again or still be curious and look them up themselves. But I knew that was not how God intended for me to handle it and taking the tablets was not enough to stump their curiosity. I needed to instill in them the value of how God saw them as His princesses and teach them to hold themselves at a standard, and then one day it clicked. Whenever the girls were a big help with whatever I may be doing, I would call them my M.V.P., which was an acronym for Most Valuable Princess. While at work during a three day fast, I was seeking the Lord's direction when the Holy Spirit tugged on my heart to write about M.V.P. As I began to write, the words flowed out of me and by the time I was finished, I had typed up the vision statement for M.V.P. as a movement. The vision was to steer every young girl from going down the path I had taken and to reveal the value within her as God's Most Valuable Princess. I was in awe because I hadn't even viewed this as a movement, but I knew it was an answered prayer regarding the passion that was birthed after the incident with my daughters.

Every morning as I drove the girls to school, we started having "Golden Nugget Moments" where we would discuss different topics based on our morning devotional. They would share their opinion and what they learned from the devotion that morning. As we continued having the discussions, my daughters started looking forward to them and I would even learn something from the topics discussed. God was using these "Golden Nugget Moments" as seeds being planted in their hearts. This was also a way to saturate their minds with God's Word and I would find ways to direct the topic back to them being God's Most Valuable Princesses.

Working in the medical field and seeing young teens coming in to get started on birth control as young as thirteen made me cringe at the very thought of these girls partaking in sexual activity so young. Not to mention the many ways they are exposed on a daily basis through television, music, social media, and even school. However, I knew this was not going to be my daughters' story. I would continue teaching them God's ways and planting seeds of purity in them by honoring God with their mind, body and soul.

Although it started as something negative trying to take hold of my daughters, I was given this beautiful way to embed positivity. My daughters were not going to identify with the ways of this world. I was more determined than ever to change the future of my daughters along with any other girl who was in need of knowing she is God's M.V.P.

# Chapter 13

# God is Doing a New Thing

January of 2015, I walked onto the campus of North Carolina Agricultural and Technical State University. I had decided to enroll in school for journalism so that I could sharpen my skills as a writer. I walked into my evening math class, after driving about an hour to Greensboro from Durham. I noticed the students that were all present in the room looked much younger than me. The instructor hadn't come into the classroom yet and while waiting, some of the students began to introduce themselves and were sharing information about the high schools they had graduated from that year.

Just a week before, I was so excited to be starting school and couldn't wait to attend my first class. But there I was the oldest in the class and had been out of high school for over ten years. I had so many emotions and I was no longer excited like I was in the beginning. I felt embarrassed, ashamed, and I knew the class was going to be extremely hard for me.

Math had never been my favorite subject; as I think back to high school I really don't know how I passed my math classes. Sitting there as the instructor started writing different forms of number factors, mixed numbers, and greatest common factor numbers, for me, it was as if she was speaking a different language. I just could not get a grip on understanding the examples she was writing. I attended the class in the evening twice a week. I was so grateful because it would give me enough time to study and get back familiar with the math work we were doing. One month went by and I still was having trouble with understanding the math.

One day, while I was in the middle of class, I got out of my seat and went to the restroom. I just couldn't take it anymore; so, I went into a bathroom stall and just cried. I started asking God what was wrong with me. I just could not retain the math we were doing and none of it was familiar to me. I started thinking about all of the marijuana I had smoked in my early twenties and wondered if that may have affected some of my ways of thinking. I started praying, asking God to restore my mind and to bring those mathematical terms back to my remembrance. When I came out of the bathroom stall, my eyes and nose were so pink from crying that I had to keep my head down as I walked back into the class, hoping no one would notice.

For the next couple of weeks there was no change. I was even receiving help from the instructor and her teacher's assistants but I was not retaining the math very well. When the instructor would inform us of the math level she expected us to be on as a class, I was always about five levels behind. I was over it, tired of being behind and I was ready to drop out. Another month passed, midterm grades were coming up and I just could not see myself catching up in time to get a passing grade. I started slacking on my work outside of school and I just did not care anymore. I started thinking school was not for me and I started to believe I made the wrong decision. Although I was doing well in my online African American History class, I did not see myself passing the math class. I decided I would finish that semester but would not return the following semester. I had scheduled an appointment with my pastor a few months before starting school because I wanted to get his advice. I wasn't sure if I should have been attending school in the first place. But after having my appointment date changed twice due to Pastor's busy schedule, I decided to go on and begin my classes.

While I was on my way to class, I received a phone call from Pastor's receptionist confirming my appointment that following Friday that I had completely forgotten about. It could not have come at a better time as I was preparing to make a decision that could possibly affect my life and later leave me with regret. That Friday, I walked into Pastor's office with a list of things to talk about. I shared with him that I had started school and but was now ready to drop out because I no longer believed it was for me. I was expecting him to agree with me by telling me I was doing the right thing but I was wrong. One thing I learned that day was my pastor was not going to give me a yes or no answer. He wanted me to make my own decision.

He recommended that I write down the pros and cons to dropping out. He let me know that continuing education is always a great decision to make. But there is one thing that he said that stuck with me to this day. He said, "There may be doors to career opportunities that Tamika can't open, but Tamika the Journalist can." He also informed me to keep seeking God on the matter as well. He had me schedule another appointment with him and bring back my list of pros and cons for dropping out of school. However, with that nugget he gave me about the doors Tamika the Journalist could open, I had already made my decision and there was no need for me to make a second appointment.

When I received an F in my math class on my midterm, I was not surprised. I knew I still had a chance of passing but that F was a wake-up call. As the next couple weeks passed, I started reaching out to Naomi, Andrea, and some of my friends. I knew if I was going to pass, I was not going to be able to do it on my own. I needed a support system. I did have family and friends that could and were willing to help me succeed. But they could not help me if I did not open my mouth to ask for help. In the beginning, part of me didn't ask for help because of pride. I didn't want anyone's help because I wanted to do it on my own. Then there was the thoughts of embarrassment, which caused me to isolate myself with feelings of loneliness. But I realized that I was in my own way; no one was blocking my success but me.

Once I made the decision to open my mouth and ask for help, I had support coming from left and right. Naomi even created an encouragement binder for me as a birthday gift. It had encouragement letters from my daughters, Andrea, my sisters, my brother, my praise dance sisters, my Bishop from our home church in Minnesota and even a letter from a friend that attended high school with me that I hadn't seen in years. There were so many other letters and I was overwhelmed with joy as I read each letter. Naomi looked at me as she put up one finger. She said, "View yourself as one finger. One finger can't do much by itself, but when you look at the other fingers that are attached and make a fist, that can make a huge impact." It was all confirmation to let me know that I was not alone.

God had given me time back to do the things I had not done when I graduated high school. Yes, I was the oldest in my classes but so what. We all have different pathways in life and I could no longer compare myself to other students in the classroom. I had a totally different lifestyle. I was a thirty year old single mother of six year old twin daughters, working fulltime, attending school part-time, and in ministry. While most of the other students were living on campus, I commuted from Durham to Greensboro twice a week, which was an hour one way. I was not the average college student, but God knew the plans He had for me. This time around, I had to learn to use time wisely. I had to learn to adjust my life in order for me to attend my classes on campus, find time to study and still help my daughters with their schoolwork. I was being stretched and going through growing pains and it was desperately needed. I believed in my heart that there was a door of opportunity ahead of me that only Tamika the Journalist could open.

I finished the semester and turned the "F" I originally had at mid-term into a "B." I was so proud of myself and grateful for the people that stepped in to help me. Due to the long commute to Greensboro from Durham, I did not return the following semester. Instead, I decided to enroll in Durham Technical College.

I started with two classes, one being an online public speaking course. In order to be graded for the class, each student had to upload speeches to YouTube that had to be completed in front of an audience. Our instructor wanted us to have at least five individuals present in each video and it had to be done in a professional setting. So, I decided to do my first speech at my job with one doctor, two nurses, a financial coordinator, and a lab technician. The topic of my speech had to be about a turning point in my life. As I stood nervously in front of my co-workers, I knew there was no turning back and that I had to do it regardless of my sweaty palms and anxious sway. I began to speak transparently about when my daughters' father was sentenced to prison. I shared how raising our daughters on my own for three and a half years was a turning point in my life. I was so nervous but I knew what I was sharing was truly a testimony of where God had brought me from. After I finished, everyone applauded and told me how inspiring my story was to them. That was the first time I had shared such a delicate piece of my life in front of people that were outside of my family. But deep down in my spirit, I knew this was just preparation for what God would use me for in the future.

I got better and better with each speech and became more and more transparent. I even did a persuasive speech regarding preventing early child exposure to pornography by revealing my own exposure as a child and an informative speech on Familial Adenomatous Polyposis (FAP), which is the cause of colon cancer in my family. After each speech, my instructor would give me great feedback on how well I did and some pointers on how to make the next speech even better. A student, who was in the online public speaking class, was also in another class I attended on campus. One day during class, she complimented me on my speeches and stated how our online instructor mentioned me and my speeches during one of her on campus classes and how she really hoped to meet me. I was so surprised that she was raving about how great my speeches were to other students. Unfortunately, the on campus class was during the hours I was at work, so I couldn't meet her in person. At the end of the semester, I finished the class with an A. My instructor wrote a long email to me regarding how well I had done in her class and how I should keep each of my speeches. I took her advice and decided to keep them as a reference to refer to for any future speeches. I truly believed this was God's way of preparing me to speak in front of many others.

After completing the semester, I did not return because I saw the big picture and realized how long it would take to complete my degree. It was going to take me a minimum of five years and the more I attended the more I believed the degree was unnecessary for what I had been called to do.

The Lord had given me instructions to write, not to become a journalist. A future as a journalist would open other doors of opportunity, but I did not want to get caught up in pursuing something God had not instructed me to pursue. The instruction was to write a book and I did not need a degree to do that. I do believe God works all things together for the good of those that love Him and are called according to His purpose. Although I had completed my semester and had no intentions of returning, I believe my speeches were not in vain so I kept them posted on YouTube. From time to time, I would check to see the number of views they received. When I would see the amount of views, I knew God was using them to plant more seeds into the hearts of many others.

God was stirring up the gifts He had placed within me and was slowly revealing my purpose. One morning, while dropping the girls off at school, a parent I had seen around the school stopped me to inform me about a group of parents that were gathering once a week to pray at the school. She asked me if I would mind being a part of it. Because I know how important and powerful prayer is, I agreed to be a part of it with no hesitation. About a week later while attending Saturday Morning Prayer at church, one of the elders that would usually lead prayer came to me and said, "God said, it's time for you to lead prayer."

My final charge regarding prayer came when one of my praise dance sisters who was now over First Lady's prayer team came to me and said the Lord placed me on her heart to be a part of their prayer team. A couple months before, God had already called me to be one of the leaders over the Singles' Ministry at my church. However, it was evident that He was beginning to stretch me in the area of prayer as well.

God was doing something new within me and placed on my heart to openly share my testimony on Facebook and Instagram every Tuesday calling it, "Talk about a Testimony Tuesday." I have shared everything, from my early exposure to pornography, overcoming my addiction to pornography, the abortion I had in the past, and many other topics others would probably not be open to sharing. I even created a blog page where I share my own experiences. I transparently share with others the many obstacles I have faced, how God has seen me through them, and how He has given me the ability to overcome them all. So many people from my church, family members, parents from my daughters' school and friends from my hometown would reach out to me and tell how much my blog posts blessed them. There are so many that were going through or had gone through the things that I was freely sharing. God was using my life as a living testimony to many others that they no longer had to put on this façade of "perfection" when they were truly hurting on the inside. I believe each testimony was literally helping free others and getting them to a place where they could openly share their own testimonies.

God was taking every ash of pain, hurt, shame, and

giving me beauty for it all through every blog I'd share, every video I posted on YouTube, and through each word on my lips when I freely shared my life story with others, allowing them to see God's glory in my life. I knew this was just the beginning of what God is doing in my life. I was confident of this very thing, that He who had begun a good work in me would complete it until the day of Jesus Christ!

God even began mending my relationship with my mother. She would call me every now and then, but nothing consistent because she was still upset that I had moved away. When her and my stepfather decided to renew their vows, I started to hear from her more and she was overly excited. After our off and on communication for the four years I had been living in North Carolina, I was shocked to hear her say she wanted me to be a part of her wedding. After over fifteen years of marriage, they were preparing to renew their vows to one another.

I flew in from North Carolina to Minnesota and stayed at my uncle's home, which was an hour away from the church where the wedding would be taking place. The day of the wedding, I was preparing my daughters, niece, my nephews, and myself for the wedding while waiting for my sister to arrive. We all were a part of the wedding and needed to be there on time. Hours had passed and my sister still had not returned. I would call her to see what was taking her so long, each time she would say she was on her way. She was in the wedding as well and still needed to get ready. When she still had not arrived, I called my uncle to pick us up. He was giving my mother away and was heading to the wedding, but turned around to head our way to pick us up. A few minutes later, my sister arrived just an hour before we were due to arrive, which meant we would make it there at the start of the wedding. I was so upset because I just knew we would miss our mother's wedding. I called my uncle so he could head back towards the church, which meant he was going to be late as well.

My sister decided she would not be in the wedding because she did not have time to get ready but wanted to get us there in time. She was driving about ninety miles per hour on the freeway. There were a few moments I thought I would have a heart attack watching her switch lanes like she was in the video game, Call of Duty! Over an hour later, we were pulling up to the side of the church. The kids and I exited the vehicle, ran up to the side doors and made it just before my mother walked into the sanctuary. There she was, standing there so beautifully with my brother. As they were preparing the music she was walking down the aisle to, my mother looked at me and said, "Y'all are late!" She placed the children in front of her and my brother prepared to walk her down the aisle as my uncle had not yet arrived. I was a bridesmaid, but I had already missed walking out with the other bridesmaids and groomsmen. I told my mother that I would just sit out, but she instructed me to walk out with the flower girls. So I walked out with them as if it was planned for me to walk out with them all along. I fell right in place with the rest of the bridal party as we watched my mother and brother walk down the aisle. I was in tears seeing my mother so happy. As they made it down the aisle, my uncle finally arrived. Once my brother saw him, he walked back up the aisle as my uncle walked down just before the pastor of the church uttered the words, "Who gives away this bride?" The entire sanctuary burst out in laughter. This was truly a wedding to remember! Even though my sister was not in the wedding, she was the one who drove my mother and stepfather to their wedding reception. She later told me she was doing a lot of the "behind the scenes" work for the wedding, which caused her to arrive late picking us up. Although it was a hassle in the beginning, everything came together beautifully in the end.

At the reception, everyone ate and had a good time. My uncle even had a couple well-known music artists perform. However, the most memorable moment is when my siblings and I came together and sang a song by a popular 90s R&B female group called, "The Arms of the One Who Loves You." My mother used to sing the song to us all the time when we were younger and it brought her and my stepfather to tears. We came together in a circle with our arms wrapped around each other. I began praising God because I could feel the bond He was recreating through us in that very moment. I cannot even explain the joy that was overflowing in my heart as we continued to celebrate the rest of the evening.

The next day, I was able to hang out with my mother and stepfather before I was due to leave the following day. It was amazing to witness them recommit their love to one another. They were like newlyweds all over again as they shared stories with me of how they met. She began to open up to me about how she felt about me leaving and how it hurt her deeply. However, she expressed that she finally understood that I had to do what was best for my daughters and me. It was so refreshing to hear her say those words after yearning and praying for our relationship to be healed. Just before it was time for me to leave, she pulled me into her arms. She began to pray over me, thanking God and asking Him to take care of her granddaughters and me. I cried so hard as she held me tightly. It was just what I needed and my heart was so full. Although I came there for the wedding, I believe this moment was the very reason I was there. God was truly doing a new thing!

# Chapter 14

# Given Beauty for My Ashes

*O*ne may read this book and say "Wow, she's gone through a lot" and another may say, "This is nothing!" But this is the portion God carved out for me and instructed me to share with you. My life was shaped from the things that I was exposed to in my childhood that tried to deter me from my God given destiny. I tried to be like everybody else in my teenage life and still did not know who I was in my adulthood let alone who I was in Christ.

I was trying to find love in all the wrong places. I was lived my life carelessly as if I was promised tomorrow and gave my body away to anyone who showed me what I thought was love. I made life-altering decisions that left me mentally and emotionally abused and brokenhearted. Just five years ago, I was this broken little girl inside of an adult woman's body trying to raise my daughters. I had no idea how to help them develop when I needed developing myself. I didn't know who I was or where I was going in life, I was a wandering soul just like many others. I had ashes upon ashes of rejection, low self-esteem, abandonment, promiscuity, brokenness and so much more piled on top of me.

When God saw me, He not only saw where I was but

where He was going to take me. He already had a way of escape set up for me that my mind will never be able to articulate. When I learned to let go of my life and surrendered it to Him, things really began to change for me. It took His love to dig me out, deliver me, cleanse me and set me free. Just like the Potter that He is, He's taken me into His hands and is shaping and molding me into the woman He called me to be from the very beginning before opposition steered me down the wrong pathway. I went from brokenness to being made whole, from facing death to God's unfailing redemption. I am a better woman and mother because of Him. Now I not only know who I am but I am confident in whose I am. I am a daughter to the Father of the fatherless; I am a princess to the King of kings and I belong to Him.

Here I am, five years later walking unashamed in freedom, knowing who the Son sets free is free indeed and have been given beauty for every layer of ash. Although my story is still being written, I can declare the works of the Lord and all He has done for me. Now that I have been changed, this book was written in hopes of being a seed to help change you.

God can take every filthy ash of our lives and create beauty from it. Nothing in our lives goes unused. He takes every bit of it and turns those things we thought were a mess into a masterpiece…His masterpiece. God desires for every one of us to come back to Him. No matter how far life may take us, He searches the earth for each of His children who are wandering and helps them find their way back to Him. Nothing is hidden from Him. The same way He saw me, He sees you too. He knows you are imperfect and that is why you must allow Him to do a work in you that you cannot do yourself. There is purpose in every level of pain and there is glory in every layer of shame. There is deliverance for every situation that you have gone through. So allow God to give you beauty for your ashes!

# About the Author

*T*amika Marie was chosen for such a time as this and shares a word spoken in due season. She did not choose this task, but was chosen to be a voice for the voiceless through her transparent delivery of God giving beauty for her ashes. Her life has been simply a series of mishaps, mayhem, miracles, and majesty. She is committed to fulfilling her purpose by sharing with the world her own wounds and afflictions for the sake of their healing. She connects well with all youth, adolescent girls, and women. Her sincere prayer is that by sharing her testimony, it will help steer girls and other women from going down the wrong path and set forth a deliverance for those who are in bondage. Tamika Marie is an asset and a precious gem in the Kingdom of God. She owns all she has been and will become. She is not ashamed to share all of her, through her story written, spoken, and lived.

Tamika Marie had been serving patients for over eight years as a Certified Medical Assistant when she received instructions from God to write this book. Today, she is an author, a blogger, and posts daily words of inspiration for all ages, genders, races and backgrounds through social media. She is an Intercessor of prayer, an active member at her local church, and is a Servant Leader over their Singles' Ministry. She is a mother to her adorable twin daughters and currently resides in Durham, North Carolina.

**Contact Tamika Marie:**

**Email:** mstamikamariej@gmail.com

**Facebook:** @iammstamikamarie

**Instagram:** @mstamikamariej

**Website:** www.iamtamikamarie.com